T0208555

THRIVE!

AN ILLUSTRATED LAW OF ATTRACTION
GUIDE TO REDUCING WORRY,
OVERCOMING FRUSTRATION
AND FREEING YOUR MIND

ZEHRA MAHOON

BALBOA.
PRESS
A DIVISION OF HAY HOUSE

Balboa Press books may be ordered through booksellers or by contacting:

Balboa Press
A Division of Hay House
1663 Liberty Drive
Bloomington, IN 47403
www.balboapress.com
1 (877) 407-4847

Because of the dynamic nature of the Internet, any web addresses or
links contained in this book may have changed since publication and
may no longer be valid. The views expressed in this work are solely those
of the author and do not necessarily reflect the views of the publisher,
and the publisher hereby disclaims any responsibility for them.

The author of this book does not dispense medical advice or prescribe the use
of any technique as a form of treatment for physical, emotional, or medical
problems without the advice of a physician, either directly or indirectly. The
intent of the author is only to offer information of a general nature to help
you in your quest for emotional and spiritual well-being. In the event you use
any of the information in this book for yourself, which is your constitutional
right, the author and the publisher assume no responsibility for your actions.

Any people depicted in stock imagery provided by Getty Images are
models, and such images are being used for illustrative purposes only.
Certain stock imagery © Getty Images.

Print information available on the last page.

ISBN: 978-1-9822-0577-5 (sc)
ISBN: 978-1-9822-0578-2 (e)

Balboa Press rev. date: 06/04/2018

TABLE OF CONTENTS

"Your beliefs become your thoughts, your thoughts become your words, your words become your actions, your actions become your habits, your habits become your values, your values become your destiny"

~ Mahatma Gandhi

(Contributed by Sabina Khattak)

Acknowledgements

A big thank you to Esther & Jerry Hicks and Abraham for being my teachers and helping me to learn and grow.

Much love and appreciation for all others who are part of this co-creation.

Zehra

Credits

Editing and cover design: Kinza Mahoon

Why I wrote this book

Why me?

I've asked that question many times in the past.

The first time I asked this question was when I ran away from an abusive arranged marriage at age twenty three. Since then I have learnt that worry, anger, jealousy and other negative emotions are the cause of everything unwanted that happens to us. I have also found that most of us think on autopilot and therefore have no control over our thoughts and the resulting emotions that play havoc in our lives. This book is about sharing what I have learnt, because perhaps my perspective might be the key to helping others like me turn their lives around.

I used to try hard to be perfect, always did what my mommy told me to, and still things happened that I thought I definitely did not deserve – and then other things happened that were completely impossible and should not have happened that were absolutely wonderful.

I was confused because I couldn't decipher a pattern that would help me make good decisions so that I could be happy. I was consumed with the need to find out, because so many things just did not add up. Fairy tales had taught me that beautiful girls got the prince and turned into princesses, but in reality I saw the most beautiful girls including my mother be some of the unhappiest people I knew, and then I saw girls that my mother said were less than average in every way land the most handsome eligible matches and be deliriously happy.

I saw lots of people, including my father work really hard for a lot less than others who had less education, less skills, and less manners - and I experienced it for myself when I entered the job market.

I saw people who followed religious rituals to a fault, go through one disaster after another, including my parents, while many of those who were lax in their religious obligations were thriving and happy. It didn't make sense that all these good people were not being rewarded for being good – but both at home and at school we were taught to be good because when you were good you would be happy and you would be rewarded – in reality this was not happening. Bad, unhappy things were happening to good people and people who were not following the moral standards of society were flourishing.

I saw people get sick and die, who seemed perfectly healthy, and I saw people with what would be considered terrible eating habits and unhealthy lifestyles live very healthy and happy long lives.

I was taught that God was loving and forgiving and that if you asked from the depths of your heart, your prayers would be answered. I asked and prayed for many things that never came to pass. And I could never understand how a loving and forgiving God was also the same God who kept score, got angry, took revenge, and never forgave for he sent people to hell based simply on which religion they happened to be born in, while all the time He was the one orchestrating their birth and everything that happened to them until death. I had to find out if God was loving and forgiving or angry and vengeful or was God prone to unpredictable moods just like the humans He had created?

I read a lot, and listened to whoever cared to share their philosophy, and met many wonderful teachers who were wise and talked sense. Over time I listened to many teachers and put it all together. I found the answers to my questions and everything fit together. Even better, what I learnt could be applied to any situation for any person. I began to see the patterns in people's lives and why things were happening to them as well as to myself.

I've found that the basic ingredients of this philosophy called the Law of Attraction are just a few, but the ways in which it applies to our lives vary based on a combination of our belief systems and thoughts, and the situations in which we are co-creating or interacting with others – therefore every situation for every individual is different and is different from the same situation being faced by another individual. So in the end there are no clear cookie cutter ways of doing things. But there are clear cut ways of thinking about things.

3

This is an important distinction, because action follows thought. So if we can train our thinking we can achieve the results we want. After all, who thinks our thoughts? We do.

I am not attempting to say to you that I have the Holy Grail and I have now ascended to a different level of being. What I am saying is that my life is getting better every day because of the understanding that I have achieved and now it's all about implementation. In the beginning I struggled with implementation, because the intellectual knowing of what needs to be done is different from actually doing it. But with continued focus I have developed a couple of techniques that I think are useful beyond my own needs. So this book is an opportunity for me to share two things:

1.   Why things happen the way they do
2.   What to do about them

My objective is to make a positive impact on whoever is ready to receive this material from me. But more than anything else, I am writing this book because the process of teaching through writing and speaking gives me great joy and satisfaction – the same sort of joy that an artist feels in creating a piece of art, or an athlete feels in playing another round of a game he loves.

Much love and appreciation,

Zehra

WHY YOU SHOULD
READ THIS BOOK

You should read this book if you have been asking that question: "why? why did this happen to me? what did I do to deserve this?" because this book contains the answer to why bad things happen to good people and what to do about it.

You should read this book if you are not at the place in life where you think you should have been, where you think you deserve to be, because this book will tell you where you went wrong and what you should do about it.

You should read this book if you are consumed by worry every day, and never really sure about what will happen next in your life, because this book will teach you what worry really is and how to curb it.

The things I will share in this book will help you to trace back to why things happened in your life that you didn't want to have happen, not only that but with the knowledge you will gain you will learn how to prevent other events in your future that lead to your asking "why me?".

I think that one of the most valuable contributions in this book is the visual depiction of the Law of Attraction that was inspired during the writing of it.

In addition, I will share strategies that I have developed for myself that have helped me start understanding when I'm sabotaging myself, and how to course correct. These strategies have given me confidence and control. I know now that I have the tools to help me deal with any situation any time. My tools are easy to learn and simple to use. They work well for me, and for the scores of people with whom I have shared them over the last couple of years.

In summary, here is what you will get out of reading this book:

1. The answer to the question "why me?"
2. Tools to identify self-sabotaging behaviour
3. Strategies to help you to make the changes in your life that are necessary for you to thrive and achieve whatever you want in the future.

Let us begin!

THE NEW CAR
PHENOMENON

An interesting thing happened when I bought my first car. It was a tiny white car. Nothing really special about it, except that it was my first car.

As I drove my car out of the dealership onto the road, I noticed that there were more sporty white small cars on the road than I had ever seen before! It seemed almost as though every fourth or fifth car on the road was either white in colour or the same make of car as mine. Was it just coincidence?

I laughed as I noted the mysterious appearance of these cars on the road. I was reminded of a concept that I had studied more years ago than I care to mention. I don't recollect that my professors or psychology books had a specific name for the concept, except to call it the power of focusing. What it was, was simply that when you focus on a subject in your mind, your physical senses give more attention to it and therefore you notice more incidence of it in your environment. "What you focus on expands", or the power of focused thought.

Have you ever noticed this phenomenon at work in your life?

For example, do you find that when you hear of someone being sick, you simultaneously get more news of the same or similar type from other friends, neighbours, relatives or even strangers? I do.

I found out that Jane was diagnosed with cancer, and a few days later I heard that Michelle was away from work, and when I called her home I was told that she had been diagnosed with cancer. Then I heard colleagues at work talking about a friend who had cancer, later I heard of a string of people participating in the Run for the Cure[1] asking for pledges – I was surrounded by cancer all around me.

Sometimes it seems to me as if the whole world is conspiring together to give me more of something I did not want. I hear of one death, and then I hear of another, and another – you get the point? Last summer I heard of funerals in a row, no offence meant, but it seemed like an epidemic! Sometimes, the event in question took place many weeks or even months ago, but the news got to me relatively at the same time. It's as if I had put up a flag on top of my house to announce the fact that I was collecting bad news, so please send me more.

It's the same thing as thinking about a friend and in a few days they call or send an e-mail.

---

[1] The Run for the Cure is an annual fund raising event for cancer research in Canada.

Coincidence? I used to think so, but since then I have changed my mind. There is a strange correlation in the way I think and the results I get, and the way I see people around me thinking and the results they get. It's as if our thoughts are like magnets that attract what we think about it and show us more and more evidence of it.

Take my friend Jo; her thought was: "can I truly trust the contractors I am hiring to renovate my house?" And my friend Jo is the only person I know who has had "issues" with each and every person she hired over the two year period that it took to renovate her house. When she replaced her front door the delivery was delayed, and then the wrong door handles and locks were delivered. When she ordered a new banister the contractor disappeared with her money. When she had her roof done, it still leaked. When she had her windows done she later found out that the man had overcharged her. I thought about her experiences and wondered how one person could attract so much of what she did not want. The only way I can explain it is that because her focus was more on what could go wrong, her experience brought more of what could go wrong into her experience. It's what my mother used to say "when you go looking for trouble, you will find it".

Jo will disagree with me strongly; she will say "Zehra, I did not ask for these things to happen to me, how can I be responsible? It's just bad luck and you really can't trust people, everyone wants to take advantage of you."

I disagree. I know, as you do, and as Jo does as well, everyone does not have the same experience. Bad luck seems to follow some people around and Good Luck seems to follow others. I think that "luck" is just the word we use when we want to pass on the responsibility for our own experiences to someone or something other than ourselves.

There is another old adage that says "you create your own luck".

When we experience the same thing over and over again in life, chances are we do so because of something we are doing, because we are the only variable that is completely unique to us and our situation. For example, my friend Jack focuses on what a horrible person his ex-wife is, and in each of his interactions with her he is proven right. I am sure that if we spoke to her friends they would all tell us what a wonderful person she was. "Jack brings out the worst in her" they would say. They would be right. Jack's expectation of her would always be satisfied.

Our expectation on every subject is that silent thought we hold in our hearts, that is always satisfied. The person who thinks jobs are hard to find is right, and the person who thinks jobs are easy to find is also right.

So what is this thing we call reality?

What is a fact? What is a statistic? What is 'knock on wood' real?

THE PINK ELEPHANT
EXPERIMENT

I did not come up with the pink elephant experiment; I came across it when I was in university. One of my professors brought the experiment to class one day. Let's do the experiment together.

Please do as I say exactly:

"DO NOT, I repeat DO NOT, think of a Pink Elephant."

If you're like me and like everyone else I have experimented with, you would have had to think of a pink elephant, even conjure one up in your head, before erasing it.

This is the inherent nature of human thought. In order to not think of something we first give it our attention, and then delete it.

Try it with anything. It works the same way regardless of subject or person.

I forgot about the Pink Elephant Experiment even before I finished my MBA, and never thought of it again until recently as it represented one of the missing pieces of my puzzle.

Here it is: you cannot "NOT" want something to happen. The universe gives you the object of your focus. When you say "I don't want this" you actually energize it and bring it to you. Our thoughts are literally like magnets that bring us the object of our focus, whether we want it or not does not enter into the equation.

My dear friend David said to me "Zehra I don't want my house to sit on the market for too long" and it did. My friend Michelle said "Zehra I have seen my mother suffer with cancer most of her life, I don't want to get it" and she did. I used to say, "I hope I don't get caught in traffic" and guess what... I did.

You would agree with me that these are not negative thoughts because in thinking this way we are not asking for unwanted results. In fact, they are seemingly positive thoughts because what we are wanting is a positive result that serves us.

On the other hand, doesn't it seem to you that the things you don't want happening are by far the ones that do? Connect the Pink Elephant Experiment with the New Car Phenomenon and it all makes sense. You cannot Not think of something, and whatever you think about comes into your reality.

Every time we think a thought that involves focusing on a subject in our lives that we do not want, we are focusing our thought on it and inviting the unwanted situation, and then in the next sentence we erase that thought but we cannot erase what we have already set into motion: the pulling or energizing of the unwanted events that we did not want.

Whether it is something good or something bad, all events follow the same rule in order to come to fruition. This rule is what is called the Law of Attraction. The Law of Attraction says where ever focus goes, energy flows. Focus goes to whatever we think about. So our thoughts have magnetic power – they bring to us whatever we focus on. If we think of the having of something, it starts coming to us, and if we think of the absence of something, the absence of it is called into our lives.

GOING TO THE "DUMP"

Anything that has energy isn't static. Think about it. The whole idea of movement is based on energy transfer. We push something by transferring our energy to it. A car engine converts fuel into energy which makes the car move.

If I was riding on the highway of life in a car, then my thoughts (consisting of energy) in the form of words would be the fuel that powered the car. When I add fuel the car moves forward and goes towards the thing that I am thinking about. If I think about the absence of something I move towards the absence of it in the future. If I think about the having of something then I move towards the having of it in the future. So that means that as I sit at my desk today and think about the bills I have to pay and not enough money to pay them, then I am creating more bills to pay and not enough money to pay them in the future.

In short, if I want to create a future that looks different from today, then I must stop looking at what is before me today.

I'm not saying that we should close our eyes and walk away from our responsibilities – it wouldn't go down well to say "I really don't like my job, so I think I will look away from it now and not go to work today, because if I do then I will be thinking about it and bringing it into my future" – putting that thought into action will just create more problems than it would solve. Really what we have to do is to give less air time to what is before us and more air time to where we want to go. That dialogue sound like "going to work today and looking forward to a better job, but this one is good enough for now because it gives me the money that I need for now, soon something better will show up, it will be nice to have that job that is closer to home and pays much better – I like the sound of that". In reality most of us don't behave in either of these ways – what we do most often is to make a long list of the reasons why we don't like something: "I really hate my job – it's so hard to drag myself to the office every day. It's such a long commute and the money is hardly worth it – I hate my boss – I really hate my boss, I wish I could find another job – it's so hard to find another job – there aren't enough jobs around".

See the difference in this dialogue? See where my focus is? I have just created in my future a job and a boss to hate, a long commute and not enough money, and the fact that other jobs are hard to find – and when I step into tomorrow, I will still have what I have today in terms of my job, because that's what I keep thinking about.

The more I think about something, the more fuel I put in the car – the faster the car travels.

The more we appreciate today, the more things we will have to appreciate in the future, and the more we complain today the more we will have to complain about in the future.

The good news is, we make the choice to appreciate or complain every time we think. The bad news is, we make the choice to appreciate or complain more as a matter of habit than as a conscious decision. Most of us have no idea whether we are habitual complainers or appreciators. Most of us have our thoughts on auto-pilot.

Imagine this. You wake up on a beautiful day. The sun is shining, the temperature is just right. There is a gentle breeze. Everything is perfect. You take a look outside and decide that this is the perfect day to go to the park and enjoy the fresh air, look at the flowers blooming and enjoy the water running in the creek. So you get in your car and start driving. As you're driving you start thinking about the conversation you had with your neighbour the night before: "she was so rude – she's always rude. I wish she would move away. I can't stand her. Who does she think she is anyway – how could she say all those terrible things to my face – if I hadn't been so up-set I would have given her a piece of my mind – I would have said mind your own business you old goat – next time, I'm going to make sure she doesn't talk to me like that." As you come out of your revere you discover that you had driven on auto-pilot to the route you take every day to work, and found yourself outside the city dump. "What a waste of time" you say to yourself, and turn around and head the opposite way towards the park. By the time you get there it's getting late and you're not in the wonderful mood you were in earlier – and being at the park doesn't seem like a whole lot of fun anymore, so you end up going home.

Sound familiar?

That's what we do all day every day. We are on auto-pilot in our heads. We want good things to happen like going to the park. But the autopilot has control and we find ourselves going to the dump in our thoughts – saying things in our heads that will lead to creating a future that we don't really want to live.

The big thing for most people that I coach is that they can't spot the difference between going to the park and going to the dump until we practice together for a little bit. As a result, I've devised a little exercise that helps me to understand their habit of thought. Once we do the exercise a couple of times and I coach them through it, they become pros at it and it doesn't take long for them to start using it – and then wonderful things begin to happen for them. I'm going to show you the exercise now and teach you how to do it so that you will be a pro at it in just half an hour – not only that, you will have programmed yourself to start seeing the patterns of negative talk as you listen to others talk.

I must caution you to leave them alone – this is your time to focus on yourself and improve your life. Don't try to change them or bring them along on this journey with you – even if they happen to live with you. Make the change in yourself and your life first and others will follow when they see what you have done and want to do it for themselves. Trying to drag someone along is too much effort, let them follow on their own steam. It's the same thing as listening to a lecture in class and forgetting all of it soon as class is over, but remembering the answer to the question you asked because you really wanted to know something.

A TWO MINUTE EXERCISE TO DETERMINE HOW POSITIVE YOU REALLY ARE

Total time required: 15 minutes (for the first time doing the exercise – do the entire exercise in one sitting).

To do this exercise you will need pen and paper, a cell phone with a recording app or a voice recorder of some sort and a timer or stopwatch. Basically we need to keep time for two minutes. Here are the steps:

1. Give yourself a score for the way you are feeling just now on a scale of 1-10, 10 being best.
2. Pick a topic in your life that you feel wonderful about. If you can't find anything personal to talk about pick a pet, a child, food that you love or something in nature that you adore like trees or flowers. Write what it is at the top of a sheet of paper.

3. Set-up the timer to go off in two minutes.
4. Take a couple of deep breaths — three is a good number.
5. Visualize the subject that you have picked with your eyes closed. You can keep your eyes closed for the next step or not — it doesn't matter — whatever is most comfortable.
6. Now I want you to imagine that you are talking to me over the phone - tell me why you love this thing that you have picked to talk about, and continue talking about it for as long as you can or until the timer goes off and record your conversation.
7. Give yourself a score for how you are feeling at the end of the exercise, on a scale of 1-10, 10 being best.
8. Take a couple of deep breaths again. Have a sip of water — but don't take a very long break — continue with the exercise.
9. Next I want you to pick a subject in your life that you want to improve, flip the page over and write that down at the top of the page. Repeat steps 3-7 for this subject.
10. Now go back to your first recording, and for every sentence you hear yourself say, record on the sheet a D if you went to the dump with it and a P if you went to the park with it. Do the same for the second set of recording. Tally your results. How many Ps and Ds did you score for each subject?

Here is an example of an exercise to show you how to determine when you are going to the dump as opposed to going to the park. It is important that you do not read the example until you have recorded both your 2 minute rambles above – only then will you have gained the maximum benefit from doing the exercise.

My friend Sherry:

Favourite subject: My cat

"I love my cat, she is so beautiful. I love her colouring. I love how she comes to wake me up in the morning. I don't always want her to wake me up though – especially on Sunday mornings – I like to sleep in on Sunday mornings. She is so cute. She doesn't meow – she makes funny noises almost like chirrups – it's so cute. I love how she purrs. I love that she loves me so much. Sometimes I forget to fill up her bowl and I leave for work and when I come back in the evening I feel bad that I had forgotten but she never holds it against me – she loves me just the same. I like it when she comes to sit in my lap and I love it when she comes and sleeps with me – but I can't close my door at night because if I do that then she will come and scratch on it either to come in or to go out and she won't stop until I open the door for her – it can get annoying you know. She loves to play with the little feathery toy I got for her and she absolutely loves pipe cleaners. I love playing with her and I have so much fun taking pictures of her – she takes beautiful pictures".

Subject that needs improvement: My relationship with my husband

"I am so angry with him. I really need for him to change. He doesn't realize how hard I work and how tired I am at the end of the day. I work a full day just like him, but when I get home I still have to get dinner and make sure the kids have done their homework and try to keep the house somewhat clean. I'm so tired of picking up after him – you'd think after all these years he would know what to do – but no – he has to make a mess in the kitchen even if all he's doing is making coffee – he never cleans up after himself – and I just don't understand why he can't give up smoking – it's such a bad habit, and his clothes and all smell so bad – Oh and he snores – my God I can't stand it. If I don't go to sleep before he does, then I can't get to sleep because of it. Nothing seems to work to get rid of his snoring – it makes me feel terrible thinking it's going to be this way for the rest of my life. I have to say though, he is a good father – I'll give him that much, and he's good at his work, he's done well and we have a good home and all that, but I just wish he would share some of the house work with me – that's all".

I think it's pretty clear that the second one is mostly at the dump, but as you were reading did you spot the times when Sherry went to the dump while talking about her cat? Here is a P/D breakdown:

I love my cat, she is so beautiful. (P)

I love her colouring. (P)

I love how she comes to wake me up in the morning. (P)

I don't always want her to wake me up though – especially on Sunday mornings – I like to sleep in on Sunday mornings.

She is so cute. (P)

She doesn't meow – she chirrups – it's so cute. (P)

I love how she purrs. (P)

I love that she loves me so much. (P)

Sometimes I forget to fill up her bowl and I leave for work and when I come back in the evening I feel bad that I had forgotten but she never holds it against me – she loves me just the same. (D)

I like it when she comes to sit in my lap and I love it when she comes and sleeps with me – (P)

but I can't close my door at night because if I do that then she will come and scratch on it either to come in or to go out and she won't stop until I open the door for her. (D)

She loves to play with the little feathery toy I got for her and she absolutely loves pipe cleaners. (P)

I love playing with her and I have so much fun taking pictures of her – she takes beautiful pictures. (P)

The total P score is 11/13, which is pretty good since we are still heading in the right direction – the direction of being happy. But the thing to note is that even when we are talking and thinking about something we love, we have that little bit that we wish was different. Now let's score the second part.

I am so angry with him. (D)

I really need for him to change. (D)

He doesn't realize how hard I work and how tired I am at the end of the day. (D)

I work a full day just like him, but when I get home I still have to get dinner and make sure the kids have done their homework and try to keep the house somewhat clean. (D)

I'm so tired of picking up after him – you'd think after all these years he would know what to do – but no – (D)

he has to make a mess in the kitchen even if all he's doing is making coffee – he never cleans up after him – (D)

and I just don't understand why he can't give up smoking – it's such a bad habit, and his clothes and all smell so bad – (D)

Oh and he snores – my God I can't stand it. (D)

If I don't go to sleep before he does, then I can't get to sleep because of it. (D)

Nothing seems to work to get rid of his snoring – it makes me feel terrible thinking it's going to be this way for the rest of my life. (D)

He is a good father – I'll give him that much, (P)

and he's good at his work, (P)

he's done well and we have a good home and all that, (P)

but I just wish he would share some of the house work with me – that's all (D)

The P score for this one is 3/14 – exactly the opposite of the first happy exercise.

Go ahead, score yourself now.

When your score is low on Ps and high on Ds this means is that you're creating more of what you don't want in your future compared to what you do want. If you want your future to be different from your today, all you have to do is to start thinking thoughts that are different from the ones you are thinking just now and go to the park with the words that you use to communicate with yourself and with other people. In the example above, it means thinking about "my relationship with my husband" in a way that goes mostly to the Park, and when you do that then the things that are taking you to the dump will stop happening.

This is the ancient principle of yin and yang.

THE YIN AND
THE YANG

I always felt drawn to the ancient symbol of the yin and yang. I am sure you must have come across it at some point? If not, I have drawn it for you below. It always seemed to me that there was a message behind this symbol, but I didn't really pay much attention to it until more recently.

I've come across people using the symbol to explain that there is duality in all things: male- female, light-dark, good-evil. My interpretation of the symbol has to do with our habit of thought. I think that this symbol is a very clever representation of the contrast that exists in all things. In the words of Abraham-Hicks "in every particle of the universe, there is that which is wanted and that which is not". So as I look at the yin-yang, I see that there is contrast in all things. Winter follows summer, day follows night – if we didn't experience the one we would not appreciate the other – I guess that is the principle of duality, but in my mind it goes a step further than that. I believe that contrast between the wanted and the unwanted helps us to define our preferences more clearly so that we know more exactly what we want and what we do not want. Every time we define a preference for the way we want things to be we give birth to desire. The interesting thing is that humankind in this physical existence is never without desires. Soon as one desire is satisfied another one is born. And in my view the yin-yang represent contrast as well as how we can use and abuse contrast with our power of focus.

I remember the day I bought my first car – it was so exciting. It meant freedom, it meant independence, it meant achievement. I was ecstatic to say the least – for all of two days. Then the excitement was over. Within the year I was already looking forward to and planning what my next car would look like.

Same thing happens every time and with everything. If I get a haircut, I want a different one next time. If I get a handbag, I want another one. When I bought my first home, it was a huge deal. I remember looking at scores of places that were on sale – it was fun. As I saw all the options I could compare and decide what I wanted. I finally found the perfect place for me, and no sooner did I find it but I started to change it by renovating it, and when I was done, I was already planning what I would do different in my next home.

Our children are like that too – haven't you noticed? They will make a fuss about some toy or new thing that they want and they will talk about it and ask for it for a week, then you finally give in and get the thing for them, they play with it for all of 2 hours, after which it is lying forgotten in some corner and they are already on to the next new thing!

That's what this world is all about – it's about wanting new things by experiencing the contrast in different choices, and then closing the vibrational gap to attain the thing that we want – that's usually where we mess up.

Here's how yin-yang work.

Let's pretend that Sherry is looking for a job. It's been over six months since she started her search and nothing has happened yet. Here's an example of how she might be thinking her thoughts: "I am looking forward to finding a job and although it hasn't come yet, I know that it's on its way and when it comes it's going to be wonderful, I know I have good education and good experience, so I know that I will find something soon. The job boards are full of openings, and I am sending my applications to so many places – it's only a matter of time before I start getting calls for interviews". See how those words are taking her right to the Park. What is also happening is that she is taking a situation that is less than what she wants it to be and she is putting all her thinking power, the strength of all her focus on the glimmer of hope she is holding on to in the midst of darkness. Very much like standing in the dark half of the yin-yang and looking at the little speck of white light. The wonderful thing that happens as she looks at that small glimmer is that, the glimmer starts becoming bigger and bigger and bigger, until the glimmer is no longer a glimmer, in fact it is so big that it engulfs the darkness and now she is standing on a circle that is all white light - and on the day that happens in Sherry's thoughts she will get a fantastic job offer. She is really happy, because she is looking forward to more money coming in, and being active and doing work that she likes to do. That's how the part (small speck of white) becomes the whole. That's what is meant by "making peace with circumstances".

Let's continue with this example.

Let's assume that Sherry starts work at her new job, she is really happy and looking forward to her first pay cheque. She has a good first day at work – but the only thing is that her little cubicle is probably one of the worst ones in the whole office – it is small and cramped and stuck in a dark corner. Gone to the Dump with that right? It's also the beginning of a dark spot in the middle of the beautiful white sphere she had created when she found the job. Every day that Sherry goes to work and hates her cubicle the little dark spot keeps getting bigger, and as it get bigger Sherry is finding more things that she doesn't quite like about this new job – she starts wondering if she did the right thing, but she still likes the money that she is getting. Then one day someone is rude to her at work, and this makes Sherry really, really angry. She is fuming and going over the incident in her head over and over again, she is telling all her friends about it, and wondering all the time what she must do to teach this person a lesson. Yup! That's all the way to the Dump! Also, as she thinks and talks that small dark spot keeps getting bigger and bigger and is pushing all the beautiful white light out. More things happen, and one day there is no more white light and Sherry is standing on a sphere of black – that is also her last day at the job – they didn't really like her there she tells her friends – her boss was always playing favourites. Again the part has become the whole. It started with a little dissatisfaction with the cubicle and turned into a great big black ball that sucked all the white light out. And that is what yin-yang is all about. It is a simple reminder that whatever we choose to focus on expands and becomes our reality and our life.

The illustration below shows each negative thought as a small black ball, as the balls accumulate they start filling up the white space until there is none left.

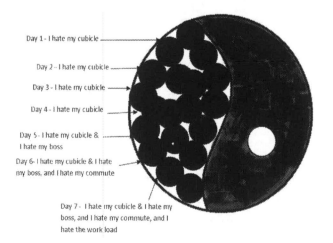

Day 1 - I hate my cubicle

Day 2 - I hate my cubicle

Day 3 - I hate my cubicle

Day 4 - I hate my cubicle

Day 5 - I hate my cubicle & I hate my boss

Day 6 - I hate my cubicle & I hate my boss, and I hate my commute

Day 7 - I hate my cubicle & I hate my boss, and I hate my commute, and I hate the work load

In every moment of every day we make the choice to direct our power of focus on different subjects, not knowing that it is like a magnifying glass that will amplify what we think about and serve it up to us eventually as our reality. In Sherry's case, when she observed that her cubicle was cramped, she experienced contrast, that let her know that she preferred more open working spaces. That part was all good, because it is good to feel contrast and give birth to desire – that really is what life is all about. When we stop feeling contrast and giving birth to new desires our time in this physical existence comes to an end.

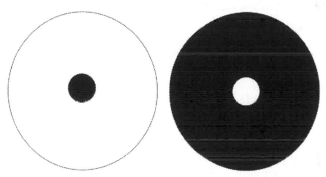

Which ever part you focus upon becomes the whole

In that moment of birthing a desire for a nicer work space Sherry had a choice to make about what to magnify with her power of focus. She could magnify her discomfort with the cubicle or she could magnify her joy on having found a job. If she had downplayed the cubicle by saying things like "I wish my cubicle was a little bigger and near a window. I like having natural light streaming in and I like more space. It's OK though, I can make do with what I have just now, I am sure that with time I will have the opportunity to move to another work station. I really appreciate having a job with work that I like doing. There are so many things I like about this company and the work I am doing, and of course it makes sense to me that this little cubicle is just my starting point here. I am sure that as I produce good results that pretty soon I will establish myself as a valuable employee and I am sure that as a nicer cubicle becomes available that I will be able to have first dibs on it – I like that thought – I think I will just close my eyes and see myself working in that large cubicle next to the window".

Can you feel how different this thought feels? And with this much of personal dialogue Sherry would have changed the course of future events. With these thoughts and words her white space would remain white and the little black speck that is her cubicle would remain a little black spec and it would never become bigger in size and would never have the power to impact her manifested reality in a negative way.

Naturally this means that when well-meaning friends and family ask Sherry about how she is liking her new job, she must at all costs avoid talking about the fact that she does not like the cubicle.

"How do you like your new job Sherry?"

"I like it very well. It's a great company to work with, and I am enjoying the work I am doing. The people are nice and I am starting to get to know them slowly. I like how well everything is organized and I like that it is easy to find my way to everything I need. I think I made the perfect decision to work here and I am looking forward to my first raise and my first promotion."

Notice the absence of cubicle talk? And notice the focus on everything that is working? It's the good stuff that we need to magnify in our lives because finding the good in our situation works to our advantage.

That's it really. It's that simple. If we could follow this way of thinking our lives would be amazing. The only requirement is to be conscious of how we're thinking and what we are saying, and over a period of time it will become a habit and we will develop the ability to do it on autopilot.

Yes, it is quite possible to go to the park on autopilot, rather than ending up at the dump! The two minute exercise is an excellent way to find out what your current autopilot is doing for you so that you can make the changes that you need to make to reprogram it. After just a few weeks of consciously going to the park, you will find that it becomes easier and easier until you don't really have to think about it with as much concentration.

It's easy to do – try it, and then observe how your life starts changing to match the change in your habit of thought.

POSSIBILITY,
PROBABILITY,
CERTAINTY

When I first started reading about the Law of Attraction it was hard for me to realize that I was doing something wrong with the way I was thinking. I thought that I was an extremely positive minded person, because the intensity with which I wanted good things to happen for me was fierce – no one wanted good things to happen in my life as much as I did, and yet, I struggled in many ways.

If someone had walked up to me fifteen or even ten years ago and told me that I was being negative, I would have thrown a fit. I would have been sure that they were under the influence … for there could be no one more positive wanting than I. I did not understand that the Law of Attraction is a magnetic force connected to our thoughts, and that it does not give us what we want, it gives us what we activate with our thoughts – our power of focus.

Let me give you an example. This morning my eleven year old was at home and wanted to bring his lunch up to his room. I stopped fussing about these things long ago – I don't have rules for my children to follow about anything. Nevertheless, as I was leaving his room having brought his food up, I had a split second thought "this is not a good idea" – I pushed it aside and carried on. A few minutes later my son was calling for me frantically wanting me to come upstairs because he had dropped some pasta on the bed! "I knew it!" I was up-set – then the thought occurred to me that I created it, and so I ended up laughing about it. I totally created it - because I activated the vibration of "not a good idea" – my son just complied with my wishes! So whose fault was it anyway? Whose fault is it when others behave in ways that we don't want them to? Whose fault is it when things happen that we don't want?

It is hard to admit and it is initially hard to understand that all of what we are living really is our own doing. But the good thing is once we start understanding it and once we start seeing the connections in how stuff happens in life it becomes so much easier to sort things out. Remember the golden rule is whatever you activate with your thought is what you will get in the future. We get what we think about, whether we like it or not.

When I finally understood this, I could make sense of all the things that happened to me in the past as well as things that were happening to my friends and people I know in the now. Often, I will hear someone mention that one of their friends was diagnosed with cancer and then in a couple of months, they themselves receive a similar diagnosis.

As children, both I and my brother went to have our eyesight checked regularly, every year. It was because both my parents were afraid that we would take after our mother who was practically blind without her corrective eyeglasses. They focused more on our having impaired vision than our having perfect vision. The result was that both my brother and I started wearing corrective lenses very early in grade school. I did the same thing with my first born, because I thought it was genetics, and she ended up wearing corrective lenses as well. Having learnt what I now know about the Law of Attraction, I did things differently with my second born. I never considered the possibility of him needing corrective lenses, although both his parents wear them. I never talked about it, I never planted the suggestion in him. I've never fussed about getting his eyesight checked, or taken him to the dentist. One time his father had him along when he went for his own eye exam and out of curiosity had him checked too only to find that he has perfect 20x20 vision – a genetic anomaly. To top it off, I explained to my daughter how Law of Attraction applied to her vision and I am so proud of her for stepping into her true power and improving her eyesight.

I can remember that my parents always worried about parking our car in front of the building where we lived – they worried that it would be vandalized. Guess what, one night an overhead electricity transmission wire broke and fell on the car, and might I mention that it was not a stormy night – just a regular peaceful night. What are the odds of something like that happening to anyone?

*That's the thing! I've realized that "we create our own odds" and our own, very **"personal probability"** based on the way we think.*

Let me explain.

At any point in time, there are countless, unlimited possibilities for what will happen next on any subject in our lives. There are possibilities that we can see, but there are many scores of possibilities that we have never thought about and many that we don't even know exist. It's like being in the centre of a bubble that is full of little lights, and each light corresponds to a possibility that can manifest. What will happen in the future depend on the amount of energy we give to a possibility by activating it with our thoughts. These possibilities are what many spiritual teachers and quantum physicists refer to as the **Field of All Possibilities**. The way we think creates, what I call "**Thought Pathways**" that lead to the Possibilities. The more we think of a Possibility occurring, the more well travelled the Thought Pathway leading to that possibility, the higher our **Personal Probability** of that possibility manifesting as a reality in our life.

Let's pick a subject to illustrate. Let's say that you need a new car because the one you have is close to the end of its useful life. Let's also say that you have money constraints and buying a new car is not in the budget just now. From where you stand a new car does not seem like a possibility, even a pre-owned vehicle of any sort does not seem like a possibility. Your dream however, is to own a brand new, deep blue, BMW.

Based on where you are on this topic, every time you think about your car the following are the thoughts that flit through your mind from time to time.

1. My car needs repair on a constant basis because it's so old. (D)
2. I don't like driving this old car, it makes me feel like a failure. (D)
3. At least I have a car to drive, it's the best I can afford at this time. (P)
4. How long do I have to wait to have a new car. (D)
5. I wish things would change so that I can get a new car. (D)
6. Anything is better than this old thing, I hate everything about it. (D)
7. I don't like the feeling of people seeing me in this contraption. (D)
8. It feels like I will never have the money to get a brand new car anyway. (D)

First of all, notice how most of the thoughts above are going to the dump? Yet, the person who is thinking these thoughts really wants good things to happen. With all their heart, what they truly want is a new car or at least a pre-owned car that is better than the one they currently own. But if they keep going to the dump in their thoughts, then the dump is what is active in their reality and that's where they are going, unless they start changing the way they think. The life we live is a barometer that tells us what sort of thoughts we are thinking. When we think empowering, happy thoughts that take us to the park on most subjects then we live lives that are mostly satisfying and when we think thoughts of worry and anxiety our lives reflect it – it's not the other way around. You see, the popular belief is that we think unhappy thoughts as a result of unhappy circumstances, but in reality somewhere along the line in this chicken and egg story we thought a thought that was negative and changed the course of our lives. But it really doesn't matter because we can start from where ever we are and decide to do it differently and our lives will change.

Let's take this a step further. Let's call this person who is wanting a new car, Charlie, and let's say that from time to time as Charlie is thinking about his dilemma of wanting a new vehicle, he starts building scenarios in his mind. Here are some of the scenarios he thinks about – sometimes he even shares these thoughts with his friends and family members:

1. My car will die one day when I'm on my way to something really important. If that happens, I don't have enough money in the bank that I could go get another car or even get this one fixed. I don't know what I will do. Maybe I could get a car loan – that's going to depend on my credit rating, plus I don't know if I can afford car payments just now – and insurance, I think that would go up as well.

2. I'm going to start saving for another car; if I put away $100 every month – how long will it take for me to have enough to put down on a pre-owned car? I really should calculate that.

3. Maybe I can borrow money from my parents, if they help me out it would make things so much easier. But what if they say "no"?

4. Wouldn't it be nice if I won a car? Maybe I can buy a ticket to a lottery that gives away cars and win! I could keep that car or I could sell it and buy a pre-owned car, then I would have some money for other things I want to do.

5. Maybe if I got another job then I could make more money, and then I would be able to get a new car.

6. What a nice thing to happen for Sam – imagine getting a gift of a brand new car – I wish something like that could happen for me too.

7. I guess I'm just going to stay stuck with this car for ever.

Charlie can only see seven alternate ways in which his reality can unfold. But he gives constant attention to number seven. So in this field of countless possibilities, for Charlie there are only seven possibilities and only one probability – number seven.

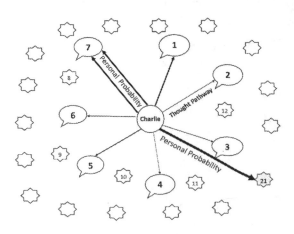

If Charlie could find a way to stop thinking about number seven, and at the same time start thinking of what he really wants: a new deep blue BMW (Possibility No. 21) without thinking of how it will come about, then with time, the thought pathway to the BMW will have broadened so much that it would become the strongest probability and eventually the only possibility that could manifest for Charlie.

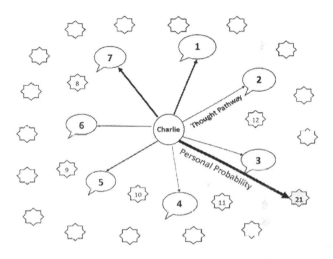

The interesting thing is that Charlie does not have to figure out all the steps that would have to happen in order to get him to the BMW. In fact, if he tried to figure out all the steps that would have to happen then he would be creating thought pathways to those steps and personal probabilities that each of those events would occur and this would take him farther away from the end result by adding may more layers of possibilities and personal probabilities. All Charlie has to do is to visualize the end result, and let the Universe or that which we call God find the way to it.

You see when you don't focus on a pathway, then the Universe has the flexibility to lead you in the easiest possible way. But when you start trying to figure out all the options you create thought pathways and when a pathway is formed it limits the availability of the other options. The more you travel a certain pathway the bigger it becomes until one day the path is a big highway that you must travel, because your attention to it has taken it from a possibility to a probability to a certainty.

The way the Universe interprets your vibrational messages in the form of your thoughts is: if you focus on it, you want it, and the Universe will always give you what you want — that is why when you ask it is always given. It is also why sometimes, bad things have to happen before good things can happen. It is because we are so used to thinking about our fears in the same breath as we think about what we want that we create a highway towards the thing we don't want and only a small path towards what we want. For example, I hear my daughter's friends say "I hope I don't fail the exam" whereas they could say "I hope I pass the exam". In both cases the end result they want is to pass the exam, but in the first instance the focus is on failing, so what is being activated is failure. This subtle difference in the way we think our thoughts and the way we speak is the underlying cause for why perfectly nice people with good intentions end up with what the world at large calls "bad luck". It's not bad luck — it's bad use of thoughts and words.

If you keep thinking about what you don't want, then you make it the pathway with the highest probability and you must travel that pathway before the Universe can take you to what you want. This is why sometimes people have to lose everything before they finally rise to the top and get everything they want. The illustration below shows what happens to Charlie when he can't help but think thought number seven over and over again. Because he gives more airtime and thinking time to this option number seven has to happen so that he can leave it behind and allow the Universe to take him through whatever hoops it needs to over a period of time in order to lead him to where he wanted to go in the first place – towards the brand new BMW.

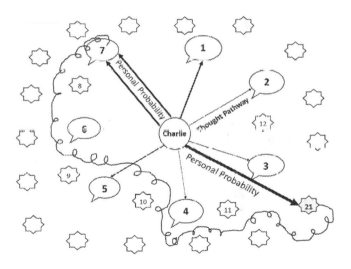

Haven't you observed those people who want something really badly and they get the exact opposite of it, but once it comes to pass they accept the situation, give up the worry and apply themselves to whatever comes to them, and then one day sometime later the thing that was so hard to get falls into their laps with surprising ease. That's when they say "better late than never".

EVERY THOUGHT
IS A PRAYER

Think about it.

If God, the Universe knows everything about everything, then God, the Universe must be listening to my every thought, not just the words I offer when I perform the ritual of praying.

That means how I think my thoughts is really important, because with every thought I am talking to God. From the time that I wake up to the time I go to bed, every thought I think is being heard.

What we are asking for is determined by the thoughts we think. If we are thinking thoughts about not having enough money, then as far as the Universe is concerned we are asking for not enough money and so the Universe answers and we have what we thought about – "not enough money". That's what the preceding section was all about – you see that's how the Universe hears us. That's why when we are grateful or appreciative it works in our favour and when we complain it goes against us. When we appreciate, the Universe gives us more things to appreciate, and when we complain the Universe give us more things to complain about.

The manner in which all our thoughts are evaluated and answered is always consistent and always fair and we are always given exactly what we are asking for.

Every thought we think is important because it has an impact on our thought pathways and our personal probabilities, and those two determine what happens in our manifested reality.

It also means, as many other teachers have said, that we can literally jump from one point in the field of possibilities to another – all we have to do is to stop thinking the thoughts we think every day and make the decision to think a totally different set of thoughts – thoughts that purposely lead us towards creating a new set of thought pathways and a corresponding set of personal probabilities. That's what all visualization is. The process of visualizing the end result we want to experience lays down the thought pathways. The more we travel these pathways the more we increase the probability of manifesting the end result that we want to experience.

In Charlie's case, if he would just focus on the joy he would experience in finally getting his BMW and driving it and forget about how it would come about, then he would leave all paths open. There would be no thought pathways and only one personal probability: No. 21, getting the BMW. This would enable the Universe to chart the shortest possible route to Charlie's end goal.

In summary, it is our job to focus on end results we want to see in our lives from a place of joy, knowing that the possibility exists – it is not our job to create the path that will take us there – that is the job of the Universe. When we create a thought pathway we exclude other paths therefore limiting our personal universe as a sub-set of the total field of possibilities.

If Charlie did not create any thought pathways, then according to the image below the Universe would be able to bring him to the BMW via the shortest path.

The prayer part of this equation is Charlie focusing on the end result he wants. Trust and faith are about him knowing that God will find a way. One way or another God, the Universe will find a way. When Charlie doesn't interfere by creating thought pathways of his own, things happen easily and smoothly and when Charlie contributes his logic to the situation, the Universe has to take the longer, winding route to bring him to the BMW.

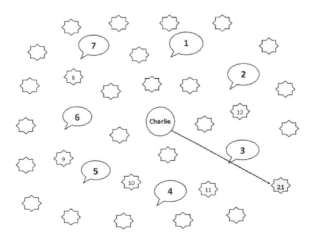

TRAPPED IN A CIRCULAR ROOM

Most of us misuse this organ that we have that we call "the brain" and that is the root of the problem we have with manifesting the things we want.

Thinking is very much like smelling or tasting or looking – everyone assumes that if you have the sensory organ then you must know how to interpret the information it collects from the world and presents to you. Just like no one told me what to do with my eyes when I was born, no one told me what to do with my brain either.

I learnt to use my intellectual ability in the same way that I learnt to use my sense of smell – by copying the adults around me. I noticed the responses my parents had to the sensory stimuli in their environment and the action they took in response and I made the decision to agree or disagree with them. Some things I agreed with and other things not so much. For example, if my mother liked oranges and I could see clearly that she was enjoying eating them, then I would try eating them and make up my mind that even though I liked the taste, I did not like the fibre that was left in my mouth after I had sucked all the juice, so I made the decision that I did not prefer oranges. I intuitively knew that I had the choice to define my own preferences. I did not have to like oranges simply because my mother liked them. But in many cases, I was told that I must defer my personal preferences and adopt what was considered socially acceptable behaviour.

The work of our sensory mechanisms is to gather data from our environment and the work of our intellect is to use that data to define our preferences for what we want. In the above example, the sensory information was accumulated through observing the visual and auditory clues that my mother enjoyed oranges. Feeling how they felt in my mouth, and tasting how they tasted. Then all that information was processed for me to come to the conclusion that oranges were not my favourite fruit. Once I stated a preference I moved on. I didn't keep thinking about the oranges and saying to myself, "I hope I never eat another orange" or "I want an orange that doesn't have so much fibre – where is it, when will I find it, I must have it".

That's generally the way we are supposed to process everything. Charlie would have looked at cars old and new, with different features and decided what he preferred. Once he decided what he preferred then he has to get his thinking mechanism out of the way, because as long as he keeps asking the questions "how will I get it?", "when will I get it?" "which one will I be able to afford?" he will remain stuck because when he asks those questions he is really saying, I don't have the car I want. The Universe gives him exactly what he is thinking about "not having the car he wants".

The biggest misuse of our power to think is making a long list of pros and cons, or a list of what is in our favour and what is not and going over the list again and again and again.

The problem lies in going over things over and over because in that process we increase our personal probability of all those events that are on the cons side of our list, because that is the tendency most of us have – and that is what all worry is. That's why worry is a bad thing – worry builds thought pathways and then we keep travelling them increasing our personal probabilities of all the things that we don't really want to see happen.

It is not to our advantage to make a list of the cons of any situation we are considering, and certainly not Ok to keep going over the cons side of the list over and over again. Making the list is the process of stating our preferences and by doing so we lay the pathways to the things we want as well as the things we don't want – that in itself is fine, what is not fine is to spend too much time considering the negative side of the list. All we must do is to stay focused on what we prefer and pay no attention to what we do not want. Make sense?

Often we want things to happen in a certain way because we think that we will be the happiest under those conditions. However, we forget that it's the end result that makes us happy and that there can be many pathways to that end result. "There are many ways to skin a cat" as they say.

When we pick the conditions that we think will make us the happiest, at times we have worry associated with those conditions which creates roadblocks to our being able to get what we want – but we keep wanting.

Sometimes we feel that the treasure we are looking for is behind a certain door and if we can just get the key to that door then we will be able to retrieve our treasure and be happy ever after. I had a dream one night of being in a circular room with many doors. In my dream I knew that there was a huge treasure hidden behind one of the doors. So I ran up to the door and tried to open it, but it was locked firmly. It would not budge. I tried putting all my weight against it in the hopes of breaking it down – but nothing happened. I kept trying and after a while I was so tired that I sat dejected – my back against the door. Then I heard a voice in my head, it said "why not try the other doors and see what's behind them". I didn't really feel that it would be of benefit to me, since I was positive that the treasure that I wanted was behind the one door, but I had nothing to lose at this point so I tried another door, it opened easily. To my disappointment there was nothing behind it, just a passage leading into the darkness. Then I tried another door and found that it too led into the same passage, and the next and the next and the next – all the doors led into the same passage. Reluctantly I stepped into the passage to see where it led. I walked only a few paces when I saw a golden light. I ran towards the light, and found that it was coming from the treasure that I was looking for! That passage connected all the doors at the back and led me to the very treasure that I was working so hard to get. If I had only stopped working so hard on beating down that one door and allowed myself to go through anyone of the other doors, they would have led me to my treasure much faster and I would not have suffered the frustration and disappointment I had felt in trying unsuccessfully to beat down that one door.

This is what happens to us in life. We think we want something, and we make up our minds as to how it will come. In that process we forget that we cannot see the complete field of possibilities, and that we are much better letting the Universe decide the path of least resistance and least number of obstacles for us.

Let me explain again with Charlie's help.

Let's say that Charlie is dreaming of a certain person as his life partner. Every time he sees this person he feels the power of his wanting. But they don't want to have anything to do with him. Charlie feels that this is the only person in the world who is the perfect answer to all his dreams about what a life partner should be. He feels that he will never be happy until he wins the affection of this one person. So Charlie starts working hard on getting this person's attention. He tries to make himself available for all events he knows his beloved may be attending. He goes out of his way to dress and act in a way that might attract his beloved's attention – but to no avail. In doing so Charlie is behaving very much like I did in my dream.

I drew a simplistic diagram to show you what I mean.

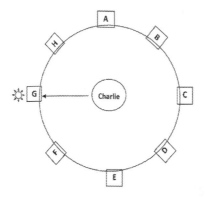

After trying for over an year, Charlie finally gives up. He is disappointed and dejected, and can't understand what is wrong. After a while, Charlie's friends encourage him to start dating other people. He doesn't want to because he doesn't think anyone will ever come up to the same standard, but still he starts going out again. One day many months later, when he was least expecting it, he bumps into his beloved again. This time everything is different. His beloved is much friendlier towards him and they hit it off like they never did before.

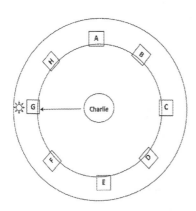

Haven't you heard of similar stories where people stopped struggling to get the one thing they thought would make them deliriously happy and then they got the very thing? The one area where I have heard of this sort of thing again and again is with couples who are trying to have a baby. They try and try and try and nothing happens, then they stop trying or they adopt, and the next thing you know they are pregnant!

I've seen people fuss over finding a job, turning away from work that is right there in front of them while they wait for the perfect job to show up – and they keep waiting for a very long time. Finally they give up, and take whatever is there only to find that it leads to exactly what they wanted and better.

Sometimes the path we think we want to take is fraught with difficulties – it is not the path of ease and flow. Source keeps calling us to another path but we don't go, because we think it's a lesser option, and yet it is probably a path that has the ability to lead us to the things we want with far less effort than the path of our own choosing.

Is there something in your life that you have been wanting for a very long time? Try giving up on it. Try to let go and allow the Universe to lead you to whatever is the easiest path to follow and watch how quickly things will turn around. Just focus on the end result you want and what it will feel like to achieve that goal.

THE DEVIL IS IN
THE DETAIL

For the longest time I thought that I needed to be extremely specific in describing what I wanted. If it was a house, then I needed to define exactly what it would look like, if it was a car, I needed to know make, model, colour and interior. If I set-up goals like reducing weight or reaching a sales target, not only did I have to state in specific terms what my goal was, I also had to lay out a detailed plan of action for attaining my goal.

How much detail does the Universe really need in order to give me what I want?

The correct answer is "none" – in the sense that I don't need to sit down and make a long list of all the characteristics I want in my spouse, any more than I need to define all the features I want in a car or a house or a job or whatever.

As I was leaving the meditation class I teach earlier tonight, I walked out with one of the participants. She was asking me questions about manifesting a house, and telling me how she was unable to find what she wanted. She said that she had written down a detailed list of all the features she was looking for and it was proving to be an impossible task. "Why don't you just ask the Universe to give you a house that you will be happy with?" I asked her. She was taken aback by my recommendation. "But if I don't tell the Universe what I want, I'll end up getting something that I don't want" she said. Think about it for a minute.

If you agree with what I've been telling you thus far, then you agree that the Universe hears your every thought – right? Well, let me add – it's been hearing your every thought since you were born. Every time you thought about a living space and defined your preference about what you liked and what you didn't like, the Universe made a note of it. The Universe also noted the intensity with which you defined your preference, and it also knows how important that specific feature is to you today. For example, let's say when you were younger you observed someone who was rough with their partner, you defined a preference for a partner who would be gentle, and then you forgot about that incident and how you felt – but the Universe did not forget. Now when you feel attracted towards someone and you think they would be the perfect partner for you, but somehow it doesn't come together for you and you wonder why. One reason might be that the Universe knows that this person does not have the capacity to yield the sort of gentleness that you prefer, and therefore the Universe is trying to lead you to someone who would be a perfect match to your desire, but you're not going because you don't see the match.

This is just another way of saying "let the Universe manage the field of possibilities", it is much better equipped for that job compared to any of us because it is the best search engine in all of creation. Besides, aren't all the details of a situation just supposed to make us happy in the end? So if we ask the Universe to give us that which makes us happy – doesn't that do the job? Why worry about what will show up – why not trust that what does show up will be the right thing, person or event for us.

My young police officer friend thinks I'm crazy – but that's the philosophy I follow in my life. A couple of years ago when I made the decision to stay at home to care for my elderly father, I started renting rooms in my home to give me the income I needed to maintain a stable base. I would put an ad on an on-line board and trust that whoever showed up in response was going to be the perfect renter. I never bothered with doing police checks, never ran a credit check, never did any written documentation and in many cases never asked for a deposit and things have been absolutely perfect!

Getting too detailed with our creation has two disadvantages: one it keeps us focused on what we see rather than what we feel, and number two because we see the details we compare what we see (which is only one perspective of the picture rather than the whole picture) with the list we've made (which is also incomplete because we have forgotten preferences we set forth earlier over the years, that the Universe knows are still important to us) – so you see we can't really compare and because we can't really compare, we shouldn't really compare. Any comparison we do will not go well because we just don't have a full view. Instead if we make up our minds to be happy with what ever comes because it must be a milestone on the path to what we want, then nothing can ever go wrong, because literally speaking we really always are on our way.

I often say that you can take out the trash kicking and screaming or whistling a tune – in either case it must be done, so why not choose whistling and have fun along the way?

Just make the best of this moment.

I count myself fortunate because this is a lesson I learnt earlier on. My parents believed that parents knew best and good children listened. Since it was my desire to be a good child – I listened and went with the flow. I did not push back. Let me share a few examples that I find rather amusing from my vantage point today. When I was in grade six my father had the opportunity to go overseas on a four year contract. We accompanied him and moved to Tehran, Iran. There were no English language girls schools in Tehran – at least none that my parents could afford, so the decision was made that for the very first time in my life, I would have to attend a co-ed school. My mother lay down some rules before hand – one of the rules was that I must not talk to or be friends with any of the boys at school; another rule was that I must never look at them. I attended school for four years and never learnt the names of any of the boys in my class, and have no memory of who they were and what they looked like. As I look back now, I am quite surprised that I obeyed my mother so completely – after all, she never came to school with me, so I didn't have to. Did it make school unpleasant for me? Not at all. I enjoyed school and excelled at my studies. I could have decided that my mother's rules were too constrictive and pushed back or not complied – but I chose to go with the flow and take the easy way out – in fact, I never questioned them even for a moment. Similarly, when I went to high school, my parents picked what I should study, and I made the decision to enjoy school and do well – it worked perfectly!

If I had pushed back, and refused to allow my parents to make decisions for me, it would just have resulted in my putting more preferences out to the Universe with more energy, and I wouldn't have had as smooth a ride – but nothing would have gone terribly wrong either way. I look back now and understand that it was the circular room with the doors back then too – only I never tried to break down the door. I just took the easy way out of the room and found ways to enjoy the journey. And this brings me to a very important subject – appreciation, and why it is so important.

THE KEY TO A HAPPY LIFE

"An attitude of gratitude" – I think those are perfect words. Byron Katie calls it "loving what is", Abraham calls it "happy where I am and eager for more". The key to a happy life is "appreciation".

I didn't really understand the value of the feeling of appreciation and love until recently. That's when I understood that paying lip service to the words is different from feeling the feeling, and that the power of appreciation lies in feeling the emotion of love and appreciation.

In our busy day to day lives we talk about love without connecting with the feeling of love. I stand guilty of such behaviour.

Saying "I love you baby" on the phone to my daughter, or meeting a friend and saying "I missed you", I was mostly just saying the appropriate words for the occasion. Then one day I connected some dots in my understanding of the Law of Attraction and realized that the more time I spent feeling the emotion of love, the better my life would become, because the Universe would see me focused on that which creates the vibration of love and therefore, it would match me up with other things that were vibrating on the same frequency.

You see the Universe matches things, people and events up on the basis of similar vibration. That's the sorting mechanism. When we feel frustration only those people, things and events are available to us that match the feeling of frustration. It doesn't matter that we don't want those things, people or events – they are the only one we have access to. In order for us to access things that match with the vibration of happy, we gotta get happy.

All this time I had been thinking in reverse you see. I had been thinking that when I have the job, the car, the partner, the house, the trip, da da, da da, da da, that then I would be happy. But now I get it that I have to get happy first in order for those things that will make me happy to show up. When you feel good, good things happen. So my new objective in life became looking for things to feel good about.

I started with asking "how do I feel?" and the answer was "I don't know – I guess I feel Ok". But Ok is neither here nor there – it's neither good nor bad, therefore it isn't good enough.

After asking the same question again and again over a period of time, I realized that I had forgotten how it feels to feel really, really good, and I had also forgotten what feels really, really bad. Through all that I had experienced in life I had learnt to put my feelings aside and continue as if nothing had happened – put on a brave front and just get through it all. As a result, I didn't really have a bench mark for my feelings. As I thought these thoughts I noticed that I had forgotten how to cry. My normal response towards something hurtful was to push back the tears, gulp, force a smile and carry on. So if I couldn't really tell if something felt bad, how could I tell if something else felt good? It's the contrast between the two that provides emotional guidance. I understood that the way to deal with emotions was not to push them aside because they rocked the boat, but to recognize what they were telling me and start using them as guidance. I had to allow myself to feel. At first I didn't know what to do? Should I go and watch some really sad movies and some really good comedy? I didn't have time for that, and nor was I fond of the idea. Instead I learnt from Abraham-Hicks to start asking the question "how does this feel?" about everything. I asked how it felt to wake up, to eat, to sit behind the steering wheel, to look at the sky, to go for a walk – everything. Slowly I started being able to tell the difference between what felt good and what felt bad.

I guess dulling my emotions had helped me to avoid staying in a depressed state based on the things I had encountered in life. Most people go to doctors and get antidepressants to do this for them artificially, I just figured out a way to do it without the drugs! Giving up the safety of that place where you can't get hurt isn't easy, but I was determined to start being happy again, and that meant that I had to figure out the difference between happy and sad. It took a while.

It wasn't easy for me to change my attitude overnight, even though I wanted to. I had to work on it slowly – like turning around a very large cruise ship.

I made small easy changes first. The easiest one to do was to change the way I interacted with my children. I started seeing them as they were at two or three years old when I hugged them – then I hugged the two year old rather than the twenty year old. I noticed that my children started wanting more hugs! If I was talking to them over the phone, I stopped doing other things and focused on my conversation with them, and when I said "I love you baby" I felt the love in my heart. Because I felt it, my child felt it too. The dynamics of my relationship with my children changed and I became a much happier person.

I've always preferred hugging my friends, but it was just a hug with no real emotion in it. I shifted that by putting intentionality in my hug. I wanted the person I was hugging to feel that they were important to me and that I was truly happy to see them. This meant closing my eyes and feeling the happiness viscerally in my body.

I started using the process of pre-paving offered by Abraham-Hicks and setting out my intention for going to bed and waking up. These were powerful mental switches. While going to bed I consciously told myself to relax and sleep well allowing my body to rest and recuperate. As I woke up the next day, I told myself that I would look for things to feel good about and make it a happy day. As I noticed things I liked, I focused on them more and appreciated them more.

I made the conscious decision to start appreciating the world around me and use the words "I love and appreciate" and connect with the feeling of love and appreciation as I said or thought the words, because just the words don't do anything. With practice, I started feeling a shift inside me, it felt good.

My personality started changing from being an extreme A-type, hyper active, highly strung person trying hard to stay on top of everything to a calm person who had everything under control. And that transformation in itself has been worth all the work to get there.

All of this helped me to realize the difference between going to the dump and going to the park. I started getting the evidence that my day went better when I spent more time in meditation and appreciation. So whereas in the beginning I started doing the work in order to manifest financial well-being, somewhere along the way that objective got replaced by the objective of just wanting to feel good. Making this shift was fantastic because when I made this shift and did the work to feel good, everything in my life fell into place, money, relationships, health and well-being all lined up. I started to see how the Universe did it's work. The Universe doesn't give us what we ask for, it gives us what we focus on. Therefore if we focus on things we can appreciate, then the Universe brings us more things to appreciate. It's like the Universe is saying "if you liked that, then here's more for you to like". And that is what makes appreciation so important.

When we go to the dump in our thoughts and in the things we say, we are complaining about the way things are and we feel that we are telling the Universe how we want things to be. But in reality the opposite is happening. The Universe hears us complain, and says "Ah! You're thinking about it, so you must want it – your wish is my command" – and that's how we get things we do not want.

When we say things like "I don't have enough money", our focus is on the not having of money and that's what the Universe gives us – more situations in which we don't have enough money! When we say, "I don't like that" the Universe serves up more things that we will not like. I see this most often in relationships. Find one little thing about someone you work with or someone you live with that you wish was different and they will show you more things not to like.

Have you ever wondered what happens to people who were madly in love and then one day they can't stand to be in the same room with each other? I've observed many such couples, and I have been one of those couples myself. When we started out, there were many things we appreciated about each other, but as time went on, for one reason or another we started noticing and thinking about the little things that we wished were different; we talked to our friends about it and asked for advice, we talked to each other about them trying to convince each other to "change", and by doing all of that we actually amplified the things we didn't like and attracted more of them until the situation became unbearable and we had to part ways. When I look back, I can't sort out how it all started, and it doesn't matter anymore, because the past has no impact on the future unless you keep thinking about it.

Knowing what I know now, I decided to use my knowledge of the Law of Attraction to improve my relationship with my ex. I changed the way I thought about him and found things to appreciate enough that we can now be good friends.

The wonderful thing about our thinking process is that we think our thoughts linearly, one at time. Two thoughts cannot occupy our heads at the very same moment. Sure, it might seem that way because we think at such a high speed, but we can only think one thought at a time. Many estimates that I have seen pin our thinking speed at anywhere between a thought every 2-3 seconds on average. Therefore, if we make the decision to think thoughts of appreciation and become conscious of what we are thinking in any one moment we can raise our vibration, because life is now, because in this moment I control where to point my power of focus and that ability to point is my biggest asset when I use it properly and my biggest liability when I don't.

Let me give you an example: let's say I am upset with my son for having done something that I don't approve of, like opening a bottle of nail varnish and painting my white carpet with it (he did that when he was two). Boy, Oh Boy! Was I angry – in that moment when I was angry could I be loving as well? The answer is No. I felt dismay as I saw my carpet, then I felt anger, and shouted at him, then felt revenge because I wanted to kill him, then I felt frustration thinking about cleaning up that mess, then I saw big tears welling up in his big eyes and knew it wasn't his fault and said to myself "well I'll just have to figure it out" with a positive attitude, and finally I felt love for him, and looked at what he had done and smiled. Notice, how with every second of time passing, I kept feeling just a little bit better until I got back to a place of love? In any one moment, I only thought one thought, but with every thought I felt a little better.

This process of feeling emotions that are just a little bit better is what Abraham-Hicks call going up the "emotional scale". Which means that it's Ok to feel the anger, and the revenge and the frustration as long as we don't get stuck with them, as long as we keep moving towards emotions that feel just a little bit better. It is important not to take action from a place of negative emotion – because if I really acted from a place of revenge and hit someone (my son in the example above), that would just make things worse and in the process I would be creating future guilt for myself, which is also a negative emotion

I could also go around telling everyone about what happened, and thinking about it over and over again, reliving the anger every time, and end up getting stuck at that place for a while. But my natural state of being is that of a loving and happy mother, so in the space of a few seconds, I went all the way from despair to love and then from a place of love, I hugged him and told him that it was going to be alright. And at that time he believed me, because I was saying it from a place of love. Imagine, if I were to try to say the same thing from a place of anger, do you think he would have believed me? Of course not. We are all readers of energy and we hear not only the words but the vibration with which those words are said. All of what we call body language is about that.

Zehra Mahoon

Do you remember when you were a child and your mother or someone else who loved you was angry with you about something and they were saying to you "I love you, but I will cut you to pieces if you do this again". In that moment, did you feel loved? I'd say from my own experience that I did not feel loved, I felt mortally scared.

So now we understand that there is a field of possibilities, which means that literally anything is possible.

We understand that when we focus on something we increase its probability of manifesting, by creating thought pathways with our power of focus.

We understand that creating these pathways limits the field of possibilities for us.

We understand that it is better if we let the Universe determine the best path to the things we want by not trying to figure out how things will happen. This means staying away from asking questions like "when will it happen?", "how will it happen?", "who will be involved?", "where is my stuff?".

We understand that the Universe uses a system of matching like vibrations, and in the field of possibilities we have access to only those possibilities that match our vibrational stance.

We understand that good things happen when we are vibrating at a frequency that is a result of feeling the emotion of love and appreciation.

The next point of clarity is in understanding the connection between our emotions and the field of possibilities.

We human beings are transmitters and receivers of energy in the form of thought waves, just like a radio station transmits radio waves. The frequencies on which thought is transmitted are the emotions that we feel. We feel emotion in response to thought and that thought is emitted from us on the emotional frequency that we are feeling in the moment. There are as many transmitting frequencies as there are human emotions, and the strength of the signal is determined by the depth of the emotion we feel. Therefore, there are many levels of joy and as many levels of despair. Predominantly joyful people attract other joyful people, things that make them happy and events that bring them joy. Predominantly unhappy people, have other unhappy people in their lives and generally things and events that make them happy are fewer. Happily, none of us are static, and we can move in the space from joy to despair by consciously picking our thoughts and gauging our "attraction" power by the way we feel as we think a thought. That is why mankind has forever been searching for joy. Anything that we do, anything that we purchase, any relationship that we have, is because we think the doing or having of it will give us joy.

This concept of the continuum of emotions from despair to joy is referred to as the "emotional scale" by Abraham-Hicks in their book Ask & it is Given, and in my mind it is the key to understanding how the Law of Attraction works. Here is a visual depiction of the emotional scale.

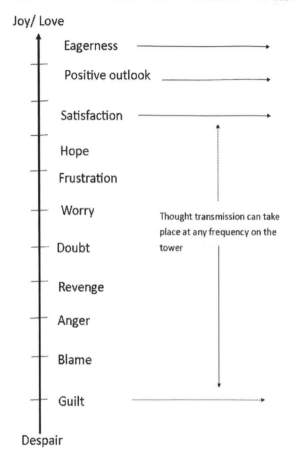

Emotional transmission tower or the emotional scale

Joy/ Love

Eagerness

Positive outlook

Satisfaction

Hope

Frustration

Worry

Doubt

Revenge

Anger

Blame

Guilt

Despair

Thought transmission can take place at any frequency on the tower

The good thing is that we are not static; we can move up and down the scale anytime, and during the course of a day depending upon what we are focusing on we could be all over the place.

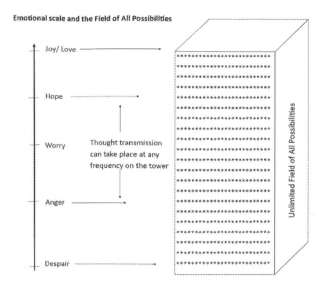

Emotional scale and the Field of All Possibilities

When we combine the emotional scale with the field of all possibilities illustrated earlier, the Law of Attraction begins to make more sense.

Imagine that you are a transmission tower with the ability to transmit thought at any emotional frequency level. Imagine that your thought has magnetic power. It reaches out and energizes an event in the field of all possibilities and pulls it towards you. Imagine the field of all possibilities as a 3-D cube with infinite layers of possible events.

When we transmit a thought, it creates a trajectory represented by the arrows in the figure above that reaches into the field of all possibilities. Like all other forms of energy such as light, heat, sound etc, thoughts also travel in a straight line created by the trajectory.

So when you transmit at the frequency of anger, you magnetize and bring to you events from the field of all possibilities that match the frequency of anger – or more things to be angry about. When you transmit thoughts at the level of joy, you magnetize and pull towards you people, things and events that will bring you more joy – all other events in the field of all possibilities are unavailable to you as represented by the figure below.

In other words, you cannot think thoughts from a place of guilt on the emotional scale and have access to an event that corresponds to the trajectory of joy.

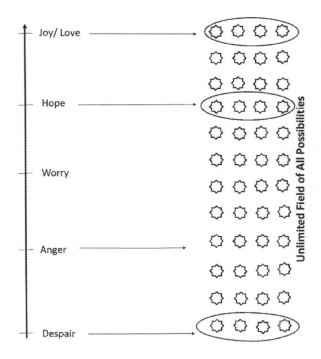

Emotional transmission tower or the emotional scale

Now, let's build this model further by adding the time continuum to it. In the physical world that we live in time goes in one direction, from past to now to the future. The past is behind us; the field of all possibilities is in our future – the next split second is the future.

In our now we could be anywhere on the emotional scale. We could be at Eagerness or at Worry or at Despair, and we would have access to only those events in the field of all possibilities that correspond to our vibrational wavelength.

In the now we have six choices about what sort of thoughts to think:

A We can think about things in our past that make us happy to think about, and adopt the attitude that if good things happened in the past then it is possible for good things to happen in the future as well. When we do so we feel good. (Going to the park) This sort of thinking process takes us up the emotional scale towards Joy and makes the events corresponding to the frequency of joy available to us from the field of all possibilities.

B We can think about things in our past that make us feel the struggle and adopt the attitude that nothing ever works out. When we think this way we feel bad. (Going to the dump). This sort of thinking process takes us down the emotional scale towards Despair and makes the events corresponding to the frequency of despair available to us from the field of all possibilities.

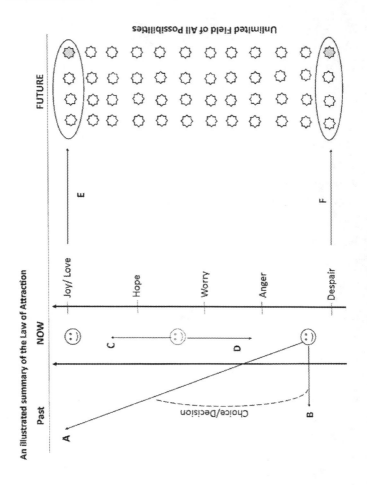

An illustrated summary of the Law of Attraction

C We can focus on something in the moment that feels good, even if it is just looking out and admiring a tree or a flower, or a bird, and adopt the attitude that this moment in time is perfect. When we do this we feel good. (Going to the park and up the emotional scale)

D We can focus on something in the moment that makes us feel bad, like listening to the news. (Going to the dump and down the emotional scale)

E We can think about the future and focus on what we want from the point of hope and eagerness of having it and feeling the joy of getting there by thinking that it is done.

F We can view the future from a point of view of despair or worry or fear of not having the thing that we want and thinking about all the things that can get in the way of our being able to get it.

Whatever feeling we choose to feel, is the key to the path that leads into the field of all possibilities at its level.

So every moment offers us a choice. We can decide to go up or down the emotional scale. I know that in the beginning it seems as though we are not in control of our thoughts and that thoughts just show up in our minds from nowhere, but this isn't true. It only feels that way because of the autopilot we have practiced into place, and we can change that by making the decision to change and then staying focused on that decision and making it a priority because that is the only way we can ensure long term success and achieve happiness in life.

Take this a step further now and combine the earlier discussion about thought pathways and probabilities. The diagram below shows how this would look. If we were at a low place on the emotional scale, let's say at a place of Despair, and from that place we are thinking about what we want, which is an event high up on the emotional scale, that event cannot be available to us because we are not a vibrational match to it. In addition, from our place of despair we keep thinking of all the things that could possibly go wrong. And if you are in a place where you have been wanting something for a while and it hasn't manifested for you, then it is certain that you have been thinking of and increasing the probability of the event that corresponds with the feeling of despair such as, "things never work out the way I want them – there is no hope for me".

The emotional distance between the thing that you want and the thing you are afraid will happen is the **vibrational or emotional gap**. This emotional gap is the reason that you don't have the things you want; it is the reason why you are not feeling the feeling of joy that you wish to feel. We can close this gap in two ways:

1. By thinking thoughts (A, C) that take us up the emotional scale, or,
2. By just letting go, giving up or turning our attention to something else in our lives that is working so that we stop thinking any and all thoughts about this subject. In doing so we will stop paving this thought pathway and with time the momentum of our negative thoughts will subside, very much in the same way as when you stop putting fuel in a car, it runs for as long as it takes for the momentum to die out and then it stops running. When we stop fuelling our thoughts with more thoughts like them, the momentum peters out and the pathway de-constructs. Make sense?

Let's play with an example. Let's say that my friend Charlie is looking for a job. There are many jobs out there that he could apply for. On the chart below they are marked as Jobs 1, 2, 3, and 4. The one he really wants is Job No. 4 – that's the one that would make him really happy. That is why Job No. 4 is lined up at the highest level of the emotional scale in line with love and joy – those are the emotions Charlie thinks he will feel if and when he lands Job No. 4. But even though Charlie wants Job No. 4 he keeps thinking thoughts that are not encouraging, like:

"There are very few jobs like that out there" (D)

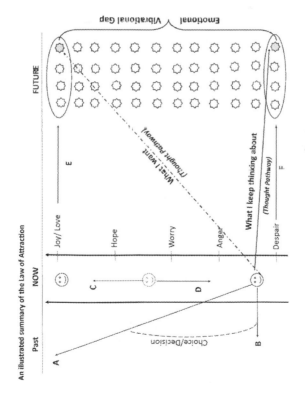

An illustrated summary of the Law of Attraction

"Why would they hire me?" (D)

"You have to get lucky with these things" (D)

"If only I had the right connections" (D)

"I still haven't figured out what they look for in a resume" (D)

"I'm not sure I have enough experience for it" (D)

"I don't really want Job No. 1 but if nothing happens soon I'll have to take it" (D)

Guess what? This sort of thinking will ensure that my friend Charlie only has one option open and that is Job No. 1. The furthest one from joy and love, the one that lines up with the way he is feeling: despair. Therefore, what he wants is very different from what he is attracting. My friend Charlie has a really big vibrational gap on the subject of finding a job.

Here's what's cool about it though. When he finally stops looking at Job No. 4 and accepts that at this time it's Ok to go with the flow and he gives up all the negative going to the dump thoughts I have listed above then many other options can open up for him. He can go to Job No. 2 or Job No. 3 or Job No.4 depending on how high he can reach on the emotional scale, and that of course is just a function of him being able to close the vibrational gap by thinking positive thoughts. Depending on how things are going for Charlie, he might think some of the following thoughts:

"It's Ok, all I have to do is to do a good job and with time I will have other opportunities come to me"

"This is great, I have some money coming in, and I can relax a little bit"

"This is just a stepping stone for me, I know that this is not my final destination, I know I am going to keep moving forward because I know I am capable and I am willing to do what it takes to get to where I want to be, and it will happen with time"

"Sometimes things take time and I'm Ok with that"

"I'm as good as anyone else who is doing this sort of job today."

"I know that from time to time such jobs do show up – all I have to do is to look out for them."

"I know of other people who were where I am today, who got there easily and quickly."

"I don't need to get there right this minute, I can wait for it and it will be fun to anticipate how it will feel when it comes."

Thoughts like these are soothing and encouraging and based on how often Charlie thinks these and similar thoughts he could go from Job No. 1 to Job No. 2, or jump to Job No. 3 or straight to Job No. 4.

The important thing in choosing what to think about is that it has to be the absolute truth. When you speak things or think things that are not really true it just widens the vibrational gap instead of helping to close it. The best way to close the vibrational emotional gap is one tiny step at a time. This is why affirmations don't work for the most part. When people pick affirmations that are too far vibrationally from where they stand on the emotional scale, those affirmations widen the vibrational gap instead of closing it, because every time you look at where you want to go you also look at where you are in comparison, without the soothing encouraging self-talk that makes your goal seem achievable. When people use affirmations that take them one step up the scale at a time, that's when affirmations work. In other words, affirmations work best in baby steps rather than quantum leaps.

Quantum leaps happen when people give up – they give up on the struggle, they give up on trying to make things happen, they give up on the negative thinking and accept where they are, and when they do that the vibrational gap closes and they are then propelled towards the thing that they wanted almost instantaneously. Things that people have been waiting for for a very long time happen when they give up – just like the couple who have been wanting a baby for a very long time, get pregnant just after they adopt a child, or the critically sick miraculously recover from an incurable disease when they start enjoying life and finding things to feel good about despite the disease.

Charlie's story

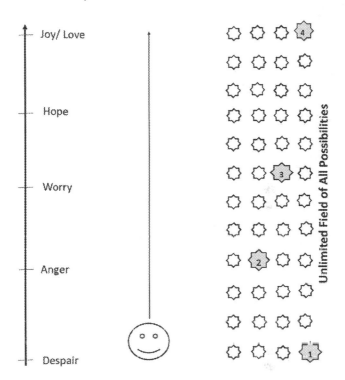

The reason, our affirmations or the statements we use to close our vibrational gap have to be absolutely true is because we cannot make a statement that goes against anything we believe – we cannot think our thoughts or live our lives outside the fence created around us by our beliefs. We have only two choices – to stay within the framework of our beliefs or to change our beliefs and release ourselves from the limitations of the fence they create around us.

In other words, negative beliefs are road blocks that prevent us from closing the vibrational gap.

So the next step for us is to explore how beliefs work, so that we can identify our road blocks and remove them from our lives forever.

WORDS ARE LIKE
ICEBERGS

Our words are like icebergs. You see the word on the surface, and it seems harmless, yet under the surface of calm waters it is connected to many beliefs that run deep, and you don't even know that they exist. If you were looking you might see some sharp edges sticking out, but for the most part they are submerged and we don't even know that they are there – yet they control our lives because your boat cannot float freely with them there. In fact, from time to time you might find yourself ship wrecked because of them and feel helpless.

Many teachers have taught ways of dealing with negative beliefs so that they lose their power over us. But what most don't teach is how to locate those negative beliefs that are holding us back. How do you find something that you don't even know exists, that you can't see, that (in most cases) you think you don't have - but it controls your life. In this book I will teach you how to use a step by step process to uncover all your negative beliefs and to turn them around so that you can sail clear blue seas without ever being concerned about another ship wreck.

Abraham-Hicks say that "beliefs are just thoughts we keep thinking"; what they really mean is that we keep our beliefs alive by living our lives according to them and by using words that act like switches turning the beliefs on.

All beliefs are is a cause and effect relationship that we establish based on our own experience and our observation of what is happening to others around us as well as to ourselves. We learn to do this as children, because we are taught straight out of the cradle that we must behave in appropriate ways "or else". "Watch where you're going or else", "sleep on time or else", "eat healthy or else", "do your chores or else", "watch your step or else" – you get the point? That's how we begin to see the world, as a construct of cause and effect relationships.

Our observation of the world is based on the collection of sensory data through our physical senses: sight, smell, taste, touch and hearing. I think interpretation of sensory data is one of those things that children learn from observing whoever is around them and from the sensations they feel in response to a sensory stimulus. Children learn what to do and how to do it from observing others around them. For example, parents tell children to wear warm clothing in cold weather. Children experience the temperature difference and their sensory mechanism confirms to them that being cold would be uncomfortable and therefore should be avoided, so they accept the parent's advice.

Children also learn how to think by observing the reactions of others around them, because every action is preceded by thought and decision about how to act. For example, in

Pakistan a cloudy day was greeted with cheer as it brought a respite from the heat. My mother loved a cloudy day, so I learnt to love cloudy days. Then I moved to Canada and observed scores of people saying how depressed they felt because it was cloudy. I would nod my head in agreement but disagree with them quietly. The decision to dislike cloudy days seems to be an agreement made by the Canadian mass consciousness, as is the decision to like cloudy days by the Pakistani mass consciousness. Interesting eh?

My Canadian friends have the choice to feel cheerful or depressed on a cloudy day and they choose depression because it is the accepted way to think and to feel in response to an overcast sky. But is feeling depressed a feeling that is desirable? Of course not. Then why does society promote it and perpetuate it? And why do "logical" people accept it? It's a "thinking virus" that has spread rampantly completely unnoticed.

It is more comfortable to follow the larger agreements in a society than to go against them. Please take a moment to imagine the look of absolute disgust I would attract if I said to my Canadian friends on an overcast day "don't you just love it – beautiful clouds, I love cloudy days". Yes, they would give me the "look" that says what's wrong with you? If I was three or four years old, that look would be sufficient to make me change my mind about how I should feel about cloudy days – but it's too late for me now!

As we observe and evaluate the world around us we start forming habits in the way we look at things. For example, my observation of the world has led me to the habit of thinking of people as falling into two main groups: 1) those who look at people, things and events as "guilty until proven innocent" or glass half empty types, and, 2) those who look at the same subjects from the point of view "innocent until proven guilty", or glass half full types. Let me give you an example.

Among my friends and acquaintances are those who voice their dread of their children turning into teenagers because they expect inappropriate and difficult behaviour from them in these years. When they talk about their children, they give me a long knowing look as if the fact that their children are in their teens explains everything. So they have labelled their children "guilty until proven innocent". This expectation of behaviour is learned. They hear other people say it, and then when they come across evidence of it, it becomes proof of fact, and then more evidence shows up so that their expectation turns into a well established belief. What is interesting to me is the fact that the only reason this group of people find the evidence that proves the fact is because the Law of Attraction will bring them what they expect or think about, because like attracts like. I didn't buy into this philosophy of teenage rebellion so my children never provided me with the evidence of it! You can read about it in the book "Is this apple from my tree?".

You see, every time someone points out evidence of something, we have the choice to accept it or not. If we accept it, it becomes our expectation and with time turns into a belief. We have beliefs about everything big or small. We, as humanity believe that the sun will rise, and that the moon will shine at night and we have the evidence of it. But we also believe in non-physical things like good and evil. And that the traffic is bad at certain times of the day, and certain people are better natured than others.

Our beliefs colour the way we look at things, they define our expectations and result in our attitude or perspective.

When we keep a thought active in our minds, such as a belief about something, our reality reflects it back to us and we keep getting the same thing again and again and again. The results we get strengthen our beliefs over and over again.

Many times we share our experiences with others, who without testing the waters themselves accept our view of the correlations between actions and situations and the corresponding results. So now more people are thinking the same thought, and experiencing the same reality; proving the correlation again and again and again, until a whole segment of the populations holds the same belief on a given subject.

The population of the world in general believes that walking barefoot on hot coal will burn their feet. Then someone like Anthony Robbins comes along who does not buy into it and proves that they can indeed do it without getting burnt. Their focused thought and their expectation is of walking unscathed over the burning coal and they do and thousands of others follow.

Whatever your belief is you will always find evidence to reinforce it. We call this proof. However, if you changed the focus of your thought and started to think a new thought, and looked for and found evidence to support this thought, you would soon create a new belief. We can choose our beliefs. We can sift through all the different beliefs we have and decide which ones we want to keep and which ones we want to discard because they do not serve us anymore. It's as simple as asking the question "which thought feels better?".

Which would you much rather believe: money is hard to earn or money is easy to come by? Haven't you noticed how some people find it hard to find a job while others have opportunities lining up outside their door?

Which would you much rather believe: I am susceptible to flue or I never get sick? Haven't you noticed how some people are always healthy even while every member of their household gets sick, they never fall victim? While there are others who are constantly visiting the doctor's office and telling everyone who will listen the details of their latest ailment.

Which would you much rather believe: I can't eat too much as I will gain weight or it doesn't matter how much I eat I am always fit? Haven't you noticed that some people eat three times as much as you and never gain weight?

Which would you much rather believe: the stock market is a dangerous place and I can lose money there or the stock market is a place of opportunities, I can make a lot of money there? Haven't you noticed how some people always win in their investments, they always find the right thing and get out at the right time, while others always get burnt?

When I started exploring this line of thought I had the hardest time identifying negative beliefs. All my life, I have been a very positive individual, so one of my main beliefs was that "I am a positive thinking individual". I did not think that I had any negative beliefs, but I was not getting the results I wanted in terms of love, life and money; this lead me to believe that there was something missing.

I kept working on finding the missing pieces to this new philosophy for life that I was developing. This led me to the discovery and understanding of the "pink elephant" and other ideas that I have shared with you earlier. As a result, I realized that I was an individual seeking "positive results" but not thinking thoughts that corresponded with those positive results on the emotional scale, and that the underlying reason for my unchanging results was my unchanging habit of thought that had its basis on the beliefs I had accumulated along the way. And so it was that I set out on a journey to find ways that would help me to identify negative beliefs and replace them with a new set of empowering beliefs that would lead me to success in all aspects of my life.

There is a disconnect between the intellectual knowing and the emotional accepting of empowering statements. These statements and whether we accept them is reflective of our underlying beliefs about life.

We accept things based on our own life experience and link events and results based on cause and effect, because we learn to make those associations due to the physical nature of this world and the reactions of others around us. For example, if I throw a ball into the air, it falls to the ground – I observed the action and the result it produced, and concluded that balls tossed into the air always fall to the ground. So I and all others including you who are reading this book are trained to create cause and affect relationships about everything we observe: people, things and events. The entire body of knowledge that we call science specifically physics and chemistry are based on this sort of creation of perceived associations. You see, whether or not an association actually exists, if you perceive that it does, then for you that association of cause and effect is real and applies to your life, until some how you come to the conclusion that there can be times when the association does not apply, and then it doesn't. Everything in life works this way.

We create associations such as: "if I don't do what my mother says she will be angry with me, and if she is angry with me then I won't feel her love for me and I want to feel her love all the time, so I must be good and do things that please her". The reality is that I don't need to create these associations. I can choose not to. I can choose to believe that my mother will love me regardless of my actions and my behaviour. Which thought feels better? That "I must alter my behaviour in order to please others so that I can be loved" or "I am a lovable person and people love me for who I am". A thought that feels better is further up on the emotional scale and gives us access to a happier set of circumstances and events on the emotional scale, and isn't that what we should be aiming for?

There are other ways in which beliefs impact us. One of my favourite stories is about going fishing with a friend. I don't fish myself, but I enjoy being in nature, so I went along. My friend who usually wears boring colours was dressed in a very bright red shirt – I couldn't help remarking: "You're going to scare the fish away with a bright colour like that", I said. "I always have good luck fishing when I wear this shirt", he said, and then proceeded to tell me a couple of stories about the success he had had in the past. This was his "lucky fishing shirt", lucky only for fishing. He wasn't really good at fishing until one day he reeled in like never before. He thought about what he had done differently compared to the other times he had been fishing, hoping to find out what the secret to his big catch was. As he compared the time when he went fishing, the tackle he used, the technique with which he cast his line, the exact spot where he fished, he found that everything was the same – exactly the same. The only thing that was different was the red shirt he was wearing – so it must be the shirt. Interesting how we are so well trained that it must be either an action or a thing that made the difference and we never consider that it might be our mental state of mind that actually made the difference. My guess is that on the day he first had that amazing success he wasn't really attached to the outcome of his fishing trip and his mood was relaxed – he was relaxed, just wanting to enjoy being out on the lake with nothing worrying him. He was generally in a good place on the emotional scale, and from that place he attracted a good catch. Then he made the association with the red shirt and now that association or belief automatically takes him up the emotional scale with respect to fishing every time the "condition" of wearing the red shirt is met. In other words, beliefs are just conditions or associations about conditions and corresponding results that we construct. Just think, isn't it just as likely that someone else might have had a totally different and opposing result – meaning they could associate wearing a red shirt to fishing as an unlucky thing to do based on their fishing results? They create the expectation, based on a belief they have constructed and they prove it to be true every time.

So if we see evidence supporting a correlation between two events, we accept it, and if we don't see evidence we tend to discard it. Sometimes, we accept and take ownership of beliefs other people have constructed – of course, this is typical of children as they accept many of the beliefs their parents offer. Anyone who has power of influence in our lives can communicate their beliefs to us – but we don't always have to accept them. Accepting someone else's belief is a decision we make – sometimes consciously and sometimes without thinking. There are times when the person is in a position of authority because of which we are convinced that whatever they offer must be right. Most children grow up thinking of their parents and teachers in this manner. When children reject the advice offered by the adults around them they experience the "consequences" of using their independent judgement, which motivates them to give up their independent ability to make decisions. Those who still don't conform are labelled "rebellious".

Over a period of time we create a framework about cause and effect in our personal space – and the world we live in conforms to the beliefs that we have picked up along the way. Therefore we limit the possibilities and the probabilities that could come to play in our lives. This ties in with the concept of the emotional scale and the field of all possibilities. A thought that is based on a negative belief feels bad and takes us low on the emotional scale and therefore the only events we have available to us in the field of all possibilities are the ones that correspond to the negative emotions based on the negative beliefs. In the same way, thoughts based on positive beliefs feel good and make available to us the corresponding set of events in the field of all possibilities. If we did not have a limiting belief system the possibilities and probabilities that could come into play in our lives at any point in time would be limitless because we would have access to the best of the best. For example, if I truly believed that money could come to me from anywhere, then the possibility that it could drop from the sky would still be a possibility that could be probable in my universe, whereas for someone who absolutely does not believe in such things, the probability of such an event would be zero. They would have eliminated the probability of the event in their personal frame of reference based on their beliefs.

Similarly, we believe in health related statements such as "my mother had cancer, so I must be more susceptible to it". Really genetics boils down to a belief system that gets reflected in the chemical structure of our bodies. Science is well on its way to proving this. For more information on this read "The biology of belief" by Bruce Lipton. The fact is that our bodies are the most responsive to all our thoughts about it and about everything else. The vibrational gap that I depicted in the illustrations earlier literally pulls us in two different directions: the direction in which we want to go and the thought pathway that we construct by repeatedly focusing on events that we actually don't want to see happening. The stress that this creates is what Abraham-Hicks calls **resistance** and it gets stored in our physical bodies first – this is a sort of warning system built into us that sends off alarms in the form of pains and aches and other indications that our thoughts are not serving us and we need to do something to change them. So going back to the example I started with about cancer – your genes may carry the coding but it doesn't need to be triggered ever unless you pull the trigger by accepting the belief that you are vulnerable to it. Your belief becomes a weak spot in your physical make-up that can be triggered by stress on any subject or accumulation of stress on many different subjects. So even though it may seem as if your genetics are causing the problem in reality it is your vibrational gap on one or many subjects. It works the same way with all diseases that are grouped together under the umbrella of hereditary problems like diabetes, and short sightedness. Think about it, not all the children of someone with diabetes become diabetic, not all the children of someone who has cancer get cancer.

The most common belief I encounter is that people with a cold spread their germs – when you are exposed to the germs you get sick. These are all examples of negative beliefs. A belief is a thought you think repeatedly and you accept as being true – true for you and the set of other people who accept the same belief. The fact, that you accept them as being true, is what matches you up with evidence to prove your belief. That is precisely why one set of medical research proves that a substance is good for you and another set of research proves exactly the opposite. It happens with food all the time. For every set of research that proves a certain food is good for you, there is an equally convincing research available to prove that it is bad! Which set of research you come across depends on your own belief systems and your place on the emotional scale. Which set of research you accept also depends on your overall belief system and your place on the emotional scale.

A negative belief that you hold on any subject becomes a weak spot in your vibrational make-up, so that when you accumulate resistance on that subject or on any subject at all, it shows up through that weak spot. Similarly, positive empowering beliefs create a shield around you that helps you deflect unwanted things.

Let me explain with the help of a few examples.

A few weeks ago I was at Costco shopping. I enjoy all the sampling that is routine there. So this one day, I saw a cluster of people gathered around one of the sampling stations. "This must be good", I thought to myself. I parked my shopping cart at the other side of the aisle so that it would not obstruct traffic, and went to grab my sample. When I returned, the woman at the sampling station where I had left my cart glared at me and said "do you have any idea what you just did?" – I was confused. The first thought in my head was "did she think I took more than one sample? Why does she have that stern tone of voice talking to me?" I just looked at her nonplussed. She said "you left your cart unattended with your purse in it, someone could have swiped it". Without thinking, I turned to her and said "that doesn't happen in my world". I saw her jaw drop but before she could say another word I sped on with my cart not wanting to engage in a discussion with her. With those words I refused to accept from her the belief that she had shared with me, because I believe that people are good at heart and all my co-creations are positive and I want to keep it that way. If I had agreed with her, I would have accepted her belief and made it my belief and then my reality would morph in a way that would prove that belief to me over and over again with stories that I would hear, events that I would witness and my personal experience. So you see how easy it is to acquire negative beliefs.

Here are a few stories that illustrate how the weak spot created by beliefs manifests in the form of sickness and poor health.

First, I will use the example of a dear friend whom I will call Jeanie. Jeanie suffered from a stroke a couple of years ago. It was pretty severe and she was totally paralyzed on one side of her body. She has recovered substantially now and has the full use of her body. She attended one of my workshops last month, and her question was, "Zehra, I had never thought of having a stroke, so how did I attract a stroke?".

At age 75 Jeanie is the most fantastic looking and active woman I have ever known. She looked perfectly healthy and happy on her 70th birthday and no one could have guessed that just a few weeks later she would have a severe stroke and be completely paralysed on the left side of her body. All the problems of her life were behind her at this stage in her life. She had been widowed at a young age and had a tough life with respect to money as a result. She also had self-esteem issues because she felt that she was unfavourably compared with her siblings. Everyone who knew Jeanie, also knew the story of her life, because she talked about it often – she was and still is a great story teller, repeating the exact dialogue that she had exchanged with people well into the past. Jeanie was and still is the life of the party telling people how she had overcome her problems – laughing all the time and putting herself at the centre of every gathering with funny accounts of her past. What she did not realize is that she was keeping the negativity of all those past experiences alive and active inside her every times she told those stories. After her 70th birthday celebration, Jeanie began talking a lot more about how age was catching up with her and her friends - noticing much more than she had done before that many people her age did not have good health. She heard of friends who had had difficult health situations to deal with, and more now than ever, she worried about maintaining good health. I would hear her say often "I don't want that" or "I hope I never get that", or "I never want to end up like that". I would often hear her repeat stories in great detail of the misfortunes that were befalling her dear friends. "Did you hear about so and so, she fell and now she needs a hip replacement…". Jeanie seemed to want to tell these stories in detail not realizing that as she told the stories she was activating the subject of ill health – and thinking about her friend's dilemmas was not a topic of conversation that took her up the emotional scale – it took her down. And even though the objective is to want a positive outcome, the thought is not a positive thought. In fact, it is a negative thought, because "I hope I never get that" is another way of saying "I am afraid of that". And fear is a negative emotion. Any thought that is connected to a negative emotion is not a positive thought. And so, unknowingly, or in her obliviousness of how the universe works, my friend Jeanie created a stroke.

These thoughts created the weak spot, and all the resistance that was accumulated in the past, used that outlet to release the pressure that had accumulated over the years.

My friend Frank broke his back during a holiday in Mexico, at the age of 35 or so. He was perfectly healthy, and seemingly happy prior to this event – so why did it happen?

Frank had told me himself that he always felt dominated by his father, and that he had low self-confidence. I also know that he was working very long hours in his business – a business that needed timely execution of orders received from clients – a business that operated on precision, where an ill executed order could potentially result in large losses. Frank continuously operated under the pressure of deadlines, and precision. Every order added to the accumulated pressure.

He told me once that it would take him a good couple of days just to shake off the tension and start enjoying his holiday, and then it would be time to go home. Just before he went on this particular holiday, he put into place a group health insurance plan for his employees. He didn't want to be included in the plan, because he never got sick. You think he spent some time thinking about and focusing on illness and what happens as a result of it as his insurance rep took him through the process of putting the insurance plan in place? With this back drop, on day two of his holiday, he decided to go surfing. He loves the water, and he is a strong swimmer. But the waves were really high that day, and the one he picked whipped him around and pinned him down – he broke his back. He does not understand why this happened – how did he create this?

First, I think that he already had some resistance accumulated from his childhood, but mostly I think that the tension from his business was still active in his mind – maybe there were orders from clients or other aspects of his business that he was still thinking about having left undone? 30 years later, he doesn't remember very clearly the specifics of the preceding events – what he does remember with extreme clarity is his journey through rehab and back to walking from a complete paralysis waist down. Given the fact that he himself stated that it took him several days into his holiday to unwind – I'm going to say that the tension of the business was active on holiday day two – accumulated from all the years of being in business. There had been some attention given to illness due to the process of putting the insurance into place, creating the weak spot. So the resistance found a crack... It really is that simple.

When something huge like that happens, the tendency is for us to find a reason that is as big – but often times, it is the slow accumulation of tension from little everyday things, and worry on a daily basis, that is unresolved and unreleased that gushes out in the form of a large event.

My friend thought that breaking his back should have been the result of a huge worry, or some other severe mental tension – what he did not realize is that it was the accumulation of a lot of little things, but things that occupied the major portion of his daily thoughts – his habit of thought was mostly of worry. He expected more things to go wrong than right, he expected more things to be hard than easy. He expected more people to be careless than careful. The balance of his habit of thought was on the negative side of the equation. My friend Jeanie, thought that she was doing everything to stay in good health and didn't seem to have any major worry in her life at this stage. It wasn't a major worry that caused her stroke. It was the habit of thought of not wanting to be sick. You see, every time you think about not wanting to be sick you are activating the thought of sickness in your mind without realizing it. So in Jeanie's case she was activating a negative thought while wanting a positive result. A habit of thinking that is most destructive. And also one that is most common. If she would instead have just asked for good health and left it at that, she would not have created the stroke.

You see it's the amount of time you spend thinking negative thoughts and not the enormity of the issue you focus on that determines the momentum with which you are propelled towards the negative or the size and magnitude of the negativity that unfolds in your life.

Take my father. He had a massive heart attack in 1985 – he was just 53. He had always been extremely healthy. But there was a history of diabetes in his family, and at the time he was just a little bit over weight. My mother pointed these "facts" out to him as she tried to stir him towards what she considered healthy food and exercise choices. Those were the good old days when the media was full of the co-relation between body weight and heart disease. Did a heart attack need to happen? Probably not. I contend that there were many people with a history of diabetes in their family and a bigger weight problem compared to my father who never suffered from a heart attack.

Two things happened in my father's case. First, he had a weak spot, created by the belief that diabetes in the family made him vulnerable to heart disease and that being overweight did the same. Second, he had a spouse who was a worrier and insisted in keeping active in both their vibrations all the tension and worry of events and people under the category of "politics in the office". Was he thinking specifically about getting a heart attack? I don't think so – but the weak spot was there and the tension was there... and the rest as they say is history.

Things you don't want don't have to happen – there don't have to be any surprises in your life – if you stay in touch with your emotional guidance.

When we think a thought that is not in our best interest, for a split second we feel the tinge of emotion that lets us know that that thought carried resistance. Most people are so used to brushing away this vital information and moving on with other thoughts that they don't take notice. Over a period of time, we get so used to feeling negative emotion and brushing it away that it becomes habit to suppress negative emotion – creating a disconnect with our natural guidance system. It's never too late to start mending the disconnect. Soon as you make the decision that you want to start paying attention to your emotional guidance – you will. If you continue to put forth your intention to listen to your emotional guidance over a period of time you will not only mend the disconnect, you will in fact make your ability to interpret that inner guidance much stronger.

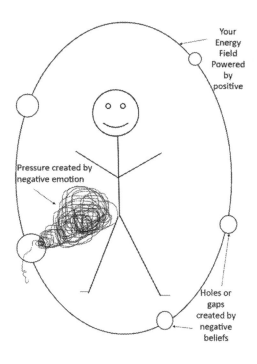

Your Energy Field Powered by positive

Pressure created by negative emotion

Holes or gaps created by negative beliefs

If you don't mind my drawing, the diagram above illustrates what I want to share.

Our positive beliefs create a sort of force field consisting of positive energy around us that doesn't let bad stuff get into our personal vibrational space, or realm. When we hear someone say something that is less than empowering, such as, "research shows that the likelihood of getting allergies in the spring is higher because of pollen in the air", and we say "really? If research has proven it – it must be true". Now, we have accepted this as true and therefore it creates a crack, or hole in our force field – that's what I refer to as a "weak spot".

Let's say you go to a party and meet someone who says, "I have terrible allergies just now – it's all that pollen in the air". "Ah!" you say "that research must be right". Now you have made that crack or weak spot in your force field a little bigger.

Every time you come across evidence that upholds the belief about pollen allergies (which of course you will, because the Law of Attraction will bring you more things that match up with what you believe), that little hole will keep getting bigger and bigger and bigger.

All the resistance that you have been accumulating, not just on one subject but a whole medley of things that have been minor every day irritancies for you, will find release through the biggest hole in your force field. Make sense?

It is at this stage that my friends get confused. The confusion arises from the fact that they had never thought of themselves as negative thinkers. They have no idea how to start identifying which thoughts are negative and how to rephrase them. How to start using language that is empowering and positive. How to consciously give up beliefs that are negative.

Here is one way to identify your habit of thought.

When you think of something that you want or some event that you want to have happen, do you ask yourself: how is it going to …? when is it going to…? who is going to…? where is it going to…? Do you use these questions as conversation starters with yourself and then paint endless scenarios in your mind about how things can work out? Do you ask the questions how? When? Who? Where? repeatedly. If you answered "yes" then my dear friend, you have work to do, because this sort of thinking pattern is indicative of a self-sabotaging habit of thought.

Tension, worry, anxiety, fear are all negative emotions – don't brush them under the carpet. Acknowledge them. Acknowledge the guidance that is telling you that you have taken the wrong fork in the road, in terms of thinking and perhaps even in terms of doing.

When you catch yourself thinking this way – stop. Acknowledge that you do not have to think these thoughts right now, this red hot minute. In this minute "All is well". Trust that there are endless possibilities and many that you could not possibly be aware of. Admit that you do not have control over all the variables involved in things working out your way – but the one thing you do control is how you think your thoughts. Say to yourself, that you want to choose positive thoughts and develop an empowering habit of thought – and you will.

One of the things I like to do is to ask the question "Why?" Why do I want this thing that I want? Why do I want things to happen in a certain way. The answer to the question Why? always takes you to the positive side of the thinking equation.

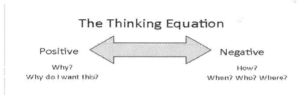

Sometimes people want to change their habit of thought but they find that they can't control their way of thinking. This is simply because thoughts have momentum. Once you get a sort of thinking habit going it gathers speed, and this makes it difficult to stop.

It's Ok to keep working on it slowly, whenever you can, and you will notice that as you make the conscious effort to change, that change will come. It's like trying to turn an ocean liner around to make it go in another direction. First you have to bring it to a stop – slowly –then turn it around, and keep going until it starts gathering speed in the new direction. So be easy on yourself. If you want it – it will come.

Zehra Mahoon

Thought always comes before action. So there is no need to act, unless the action will bring you respite, and make you feel better.

When people start understanding the Law of Attraction and how it works, often they expect that they should go from despair on the emotional scale to joy, and then stay there. When that doesn't happen, they discard the Law of Attraction and the science of deliberate creation – because they don't see the evidence of it working.

What they do not know is that, feeling respite, feeling just a little bit better than before is in fact evidence that more good stuff is on its way. What they do not know is that hardly anyone can maintain a place of consistent joy on the emotional scale, every minute of the day, day in, day out. We all experience various levels on the emotional scale during a day – success is in acknowledging when you are at the lower frequencies and then doing the work that makes you feel just a little bit better so that the direction in which you are travelling is upwards, towards joy.

How to identify negative beliefs

Beliefs are just thoughts we have accepted as being true and we think them over and over again. Most of the time, we can't really tell if we have any negative beliefs, because we all want good things to happen to us. We don't consciously want to think about things that will get in the way of our achieving our goals, but the truth is if we are not achieving the things we want in life, it is always because we are thinking about it the wrong way.

On my journey of self-improvement and growth, I have created a process that helps me to uncover and deactivate my negative beliefs with regards to any subject that I want to work on.

Basically, a negative belief is a hurdle, a blockage, but it is not something that seems big for it is just a thought. In the myriad of thoughts that go through our heads it is easy not to notice those that might be negative beliefs. In many cases we have had those negative beliefs or thoughts for such a long time that we don't notice them any more – just like the new billboard that goes up on the route to work, we only notice it the first few times we see it, and then it no longer attracts our attention and seems invisible.

As soon as we focus on a subject, all the beliefs we hold connected to it are activated. So we don't even have to think about our beliefs specifically in order to activate them! Take the example of money. If it is my belief that money is hard to earn, then every time I think about money that belief is activated. Let's say that I am in the process of making a bill payment, and I am thinking that I don't have enough money, I have activated the belief that money is hard to earn without actually thinking that thought or speaking it aloud – and that is why it is hard to spot our negative beliefs.

I've tried asking myself, "what are my negative beliefs about the subject of money?" but nothing really comes up, except a few random thoughts. I've found that a better way to come up with them is to ask the questions:

"What are my challenges?" and, "What are my fears?"

Everything I write in response to these two questions is merely a belief and a negative one. Our fears and challenges are real – it's not like we make them up, but they came from somewhere, and that somewhere is the process of observing, accepting and regurgitating a thought. Fears and challenges are just arguments that we create in our heads, and once we give them attention, then the Law of Attraction brings us the evidence that proves them to be true and more events, people and things that match those feelings start showing up in our lives. As a result, we keep thinking these negative thoughts over and over again, giving rise to worry – a negative feeling on the emotional scale. When we think negative thoughts again and again we add energy to them and increase their probability and this is how negative beliefs are born.

Thoughts of fear and difficulty can only be thought from a lower place on the emotional scale. Think about it. Can you be in a state of love and joy and at the same time feel anger, revenge, guilt and despair? Of course not. It's either one or the other. Negative emotion cannot occupy the same space and time as positive emotion. So if challenges and fears are thought of from a lower place on the emotional scale then it follows that when we think these thoughts we can only have access to that part of the field of all possibilities that corresponds to those frequencies – in other words, we cannot have access to the things we want from there. Because we keep thinking about our challenges and fears all the time, they tend to keep us at a lower place on the emotional scale. In order to get to the things we want, we have to move up the emotional scale, which means we have to resolve our fears and challenges, remove them or deactivate them.

Let's take an example to work with.

Let's say that the subject upon which I wish to accomplish improvement is my relationship with my spouse.

What are my fears?

1. My fear is that he doesn't care about me anymore.
2. My fear is that my marriage is ending.
3. My fear is that I don't know how to survive on my own if my marriage ends.

4.   My fear is that people, family and friends will say all sorts of hurtful things.
5.   My fear is that no one will really understand my situation and my feelings.
6.   My fear is that my children will be hurt – they will suffer.
7.   My fear is nothing will ever change.
8.   My fear is that things will get worse.
9.   My fear is that I will lose everything that I have created over the years.
10. My fear is that I will never be happy again.

What are my challenges?

1.   My challenge is that he doesn't listen to me.
2.   My challenge is that I don't think on my feet and give the wrong responses.
3.   My challenge is in keeping my cool when speaking with him.
4.   My challenge is trying to convince him to see things my way.
5.   My challenge is in trying to be the way I think he wants me to be.
6.   My challenge is in trying to find a way to be happy.
7.   My challenge is in trying to find things that we can do together.
8.   My challenge is to act normal so that no one finds out what's going on.
9.   My challenge is that I feel tired and drained all the time.

10. My challenge is to stop myself from crying all the time.

Once you write out your fears and challenges you have all the main beliefs that are keeping you from the things you want. Now all that remains to be done is to deactivate them so that they no longer prevent you from getting the things you want.

There are two ways to deactivate beliefs or remove them.

1. We can simply give-up all our beliefs in one swoop, and rise up the emotional scale; or
2. We can start shifting our thoughts gently, one step at a time, and slowly move up the emotional scale.

The first option is what is popularly known as a "quantum leap". Many of us experience huge shifts in our vibration at certain times in our lives when we are confronted with situations where our desire for improvement is so huge that nothing can stand in its way. For most of us, and for most situations, it is probably easier to use the second method, taking small steps to change the focus of our thoughts so that we can feel just a little bit better at each step and slowly climb up the emotional scale.

Abraham-Hicks teach many processes that help us in finding our way up the emotional scale. Using their work as the basis, I have developed what I call The Four Step Process which systematically helps to deactivate negative beliefs.

The diagram below is a visual depiction of the difference between a quantum leap and a step wise improvement using the Four Step Process. In the diagram below, the vertical axis is a measure of the intensity of an emotion also referred to as momentum throughout this book. When we spend a lot of time at a certain emotional level the intensity or pulling power of that emotion becomes higher so that it is pulling harder at the corresponding possibilities in the field of all possibilities. The Four Step Process is a stepwise reduction in the pulling power of the negative emotion that simultaneously helps us to move towards the higher emotions.

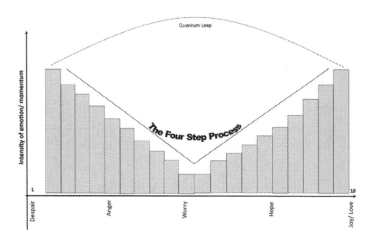

THE FOUR STEP PROCESS FOR SHIFTING BELIEFS

The Four Step Process is a simple exercise that helps us to write a few statements at a time, with the intention of improving our vibration and closing the vibrational gap.

Abraham-Hicks teach a process called the Focus Wheel, which I believe is a very useful process to help move us towards the things we want. The Four Step Process that I work with was inspired by the Focus Wheel Process. The Four Step Process not only helps to move us towards manifesting what we want, it helps us to shift our beliefs from negative beliefs about anything towards positive beliefs that we have identified as more desirable and empowering.

The objective of The Four Step Process is to help us close the vibrational gap between where we stand on a subject and where we want to go. The underlying premise behind the process is that we need to travel upwards on the emotional scale in a stepwise fashion to close the

Zehra Mahoon

vibrational gap – meaning that you cannot jump from a place of despair straight to a place of joy but that you need to go through some of the steps in between. Sometimes we can close the gap quickly and sometimes it takes a while – both are Ok because in the end what we want is that the vibrational gap be closed. The other premise behind The Four Step Process is that for the most part, we cannot maintain our position at a high place on the emotional scale for very long in the beginning and we need to keep repeating The Four Step Process in order to practice being there, and generating the momentum that will keep us there for just a little bit longer every time we go through the four steps.

To make it simpler to use the emotional scale for this exercise, I use a number scale rather than an adjective scale. Neither one is better than the other, it's just all about what feels easier – and to me personally a number scale feels easier. On the number scale "ten" represents the very top of the emotional scale, and the corresponding feeling of love and joy, and "one" represents a feeling of despair which is right at the bottom of the scale. This way I don't have to find the right adjective to describe how I feel, and I can work in relative terms. It also helps me to divide the scale into two equal halves at the "worry line", so that when you are above the worry line you are in a positive vibration area of the emotional scale and when you are below the worry line you are in the negative emotion area of the scale.

Law of Attraction Summary

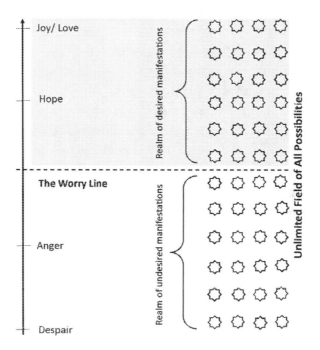

Take a look at the figure below; it helps explain what happens to us at an emotional level on a daily basis. In this example we are observing the vibrational shift in someone who starts at the level of despair on the emotional scale or at a score of one. They start doing the vibrational work or thinking exercises, making a conscious effort to shift their vibration to a higher level. This is Phase 1. For most people, starting at one and doing The Four Step Process raises their vibration on a temporary basis. They feel a little better but they are not able to hold on to the improvement and so they come back down the scale and start again almost on a daily basis. During this phase our manifestations don't change; all we accomplish is a slight shift in the way we feel. Sometimes people get discouraged because they don't see the manifestational results that confirm that they are on their way in the right direction. The missing piece is that the feeling in itself is a manifestation – it is something they have accomplished by doing the work. You see, as a group human kind has become so used to brushing aside how they feel that a shift in the way they feel doesn't seem important enough – whereas that in itself is everything. Celebrating the shift in feeling results in a further shift, and a further shift and a further shift until a positive manifestation arrives.

Notice on Day 7, even though their vibration dips during the course of the day, it doesn't go all the way down to despair. So they leave their vibration in a better place, and the next day they are able to pick it up from there and take it to a new high. The most significant thing about Phase 1 is that the vibrational gap is still pretty big so even though there are daily improvements, Phase 1 stays below the "worry line" or a score of 5 on the emotional scale. Scores of 5 and below are all under the worry line, and all that means is that our negative thoughts still have a high momentum, and are still occupying a lot of our attention. When scores start staying consistently above the worry line, it means that you now have an established habit of positive thinking and the evidence of it is beginning to show up in manifested reality. This starts happening in Phase 2, but is mostly evident in Phase 3. The most significant thing to note in Phase 2 is that even though vibration can dip pretty low, for example to C, it is now easier to do the work and so it is possible to jump from a low vibration to a relatively high vibration within the course of the same day. Note that at point C even though the dip in vibration is significant, it does not fall all the way to despair – because once we start doing the work we can never go back.

The most significant thing about Phase 3 is that it is above the worry line. Even when there is a dip in vibration, it mostly stays above the worry line.

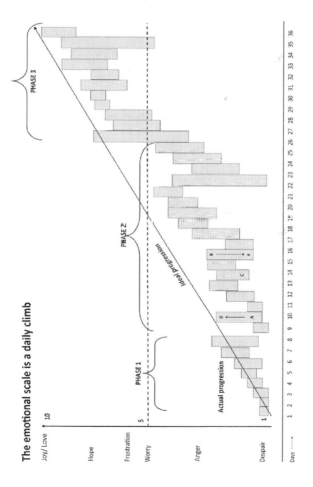

Once we get in the habit of staying above the worry line, life starts to feel good, and positive thinking becomes a habit so that even if we were to stop using The Four Step Process, we would still be able to maintain our position above the worry line. Although the amount of time it would take for anyone to get to Phase 3 is different from person to person, a pretty significant shift can take place within thirty to forty days.

Here is the outline of how The Four Step Process works. To do this exercise you need a sheet of paper and a pen.

Step One: State it the way it is

Write a statement of where you are at the top of the page. This will usually be a negative statement or will make you focus on a place that you actually want to get away from – but don't be afraid that focusing there will make the problem bigger. That only happens when you stay static in you focus. What we are going to do is to help you to move your focus in a direction that takes you up the emotional scale by generating thought energy that creates the momentum or generates the speed that you need in order to lift you from where you are. Do this step of the exercise in the same spirit in which you would enter the starting point of your journey in your GPS or a mapping service in order to figure out the route towards your final destination.

It helps to give yourself a score on the emotional scale next to the statement so that you can quantify the improvement in the way you feel at the end of the exercise. A pat on the back will help you feel even better.

Step two: State what you want

At the bottom of the sheet of paper write a clear statement of what you want. The distance between the statement on the top of the page in step one and the statement at the bottom of the page in step two is the vibrational gap that we will close in steps three and four.

There are some guidelines for writing the statement of what you want.

1. The easiest way to write the statement for step two is to word it so that it is the exact opposite of the statement in step one. This is your ultimate goal, but at any point in time you can only move one or two steps towards your goal, because it is not possible to make the jump from where you are to where you want to go in one leap – especially if you are very far from your goal. As you continue to repeat The Four Step Process, you will keep improving your energy and continue your journey up the emotional scale. For example, you pick up things from let's say being a four on the emotional scale and moving to a six. The next time you will pick it up from a six (even if you dip a little in the interim, it's unlikely that you will fall all the way to four again), and move it further up perhaps to a seven or an eight. Make sense?

2. It would be better if your statement or goal is about moving just one tiny step forward and not about getting to the final destination. So ask yourself the question "what has to happen so that I feel just a

little bit better?" and use the answer to that question for your statement.

3. Keep it general. Don't describe the details of what you want.

4. Aim for the feeling of how it will feel rather than the specifics of what you want.

Step Three: soothe yourself

The first step in feeling better is to soothe yourself. The process of soothing involves accepting where you are, forgiving yourself, justifying your anger, blaming others or circumstances. These are all emotions on the lower end of the emotional scale mostly below the worry line. Society teaches us that it is wrong to express these sorts of emotions and the usual tendency is to try to curb them – but pushing back against a negative emotion in the hope that it will go away only serves to make it bigger.

I have come to understand that it is not that society thinks it is bad to feel the negative emotion but that it is bad to act on them. So if you feel anger, instead of demonstrating it, you should curb it – suck it up. Law of Attraction agrees. It's Ok to feel the feeling of revenge and think vengeful thoughts, but acting on those thoughts would not help us to get back to the place of joy and love that is our final destination. Feeling anger is Ok, but to act from a place of anger will only lead to a feeling of regret later which is very close to blame – just a notch above despair at the very bottom of the emotional scale. Law of Attraction teaches us that it is in fact important to feel the negative emotions as they come and let them go without acting on them, while congratulating yourself for moving up the emotional scale. It's only when we get stuck at a low place of the emotional scale and continue to wallow in negative emotion that things truly go wrong.

Step Four: close the vibrational gap

We close the gap by making at least five to ten statements or thoughts that take us up the emotional scale. The criteria for constructing suitable statements are:

1. The statements are worded in a way that "feels" better than the statement from step one. They soften the feeling or emotion expressed in step one.
2. We have the choice to pick any of the possible six types of thoughts (A, B, C, D, E, F from the earlier section on six thinking choices in the chapter: The key to a happy life), but we have to make the decision to pick only those types of thoughts that are positive and will take us up the emotional scale. This means we can pick a mix of thoughts from the following types: A, C, and E – meaning that we can search for a better feeling thought from the past, present or future.
3. The statements are absolutely true.
4. Use wording for your last statement that bridges over to the statement at the bottom of the page from step two.

Doing the Four Step Process once or twice is not enough. Repeat the process until you are able to get to phase three and hang out consistently above the worry line.

SHIFTING NEGATIVE BELIEFS

Each one of our fears and challenges identified earlier is a negative belief that we can work on using The Four Step Process. Doing this reduces the hold that the negative belief has on us, and we feel better because some of the pressure caused by the accumulation of resistance inside us is relieved. Work through each challenge and fear using The Four Step Process.

Every time you do this exercise, it will create a shift upwards on the emotional scale. It is best to discard the worksheets as you complete them. Going back to read your work will activate the vibration of where you were when you did the work, and there is no need for that because in most cases that will mean going backward – and there is really only one way to go and that is forward. Because who you are today is not exactly the same as who you were yesterday, or the day before, or the day before that. You are continuously changing in every moment, and in this moment here and now you have the opportunity to create who you will be in the next moment, the next hour, and the next day.

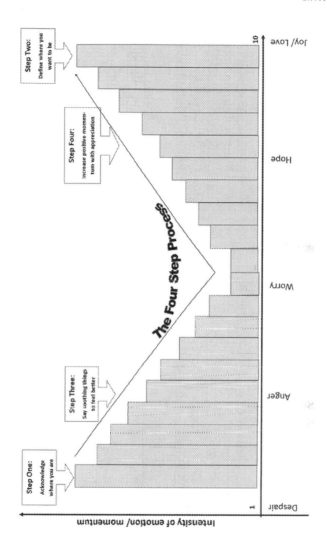

In the following sections I will share with you samples of how to apply The Four Step Process to the subjects of relationships, money, health and self-worth. The objective is to show you how to do the exercise from various perspectives, just your reading of the exercises is not enough to help create a vibrational shift for you, although it will, but the shift that you will feel when you do the work yourself will be so much more powerful. ***Doing the work is more powerful than reading about doing the work.***

Lastly, we have a tendency to skip ahead and get straight to the subject that concerns us the most. Someone who has challenges and fears mostly about money may decide that they want to skip ahead to The Four Step Process about money and not spend time reading the other samples. Where there is no harm in skipping ahead – do remember to come back and read the other examples, because these will help you get better acquainted with doing the process and changing your practised way of thinking. The objective here is to learn how to think, and a variety of examples will help to do just that.

Here's a way to tell if the work you've done with the Four Step Process has been effective in shifting your beliefs – it's called muscle testing, and is quite widely used in many different ways.

The basic premise behind muscle testing is that our bodies are very sensitive to the thoughts we think. When we think thoughts that are above the worry line our bodies respond in healthy ways that support our well-being and when we think thoughts from an emotional point below the worry line our bodies respond in ways that do not support our well-being. That's why worry and anxiety result in health problems. Our bodies are chemical factories that manufacture chemicals in the form of enzymes that we need to digest our food and perform various body functions. Emotions below the worry line disrupt the normal chemical production and result in the production of harmful substances, while emotions above the worry line support the well-being of our bodies. So when we tell a lie, or say something that we don't really believe is true our bodies react in a manner that makes them weaker, so our muscle strength is reduced.

Muscle testing is especially helpful for people who have lost the ability to interpret where they are on the emotional scale and are therefore unable to tell the difference between feeling good or feeling bad, because to them everything feels Ok. In other words they have trained themselves to not feel too much joy or too much pain so that they can function in society without throwing tantrums.

A muscle test requires two people: the person doing the test and a facilitator. Here's an outline of how muscle testing works.

1. The person doing the test stands straight consciously thinking about feeling relaxed. It is helpful to make sure that your chin is aligned with your neck so that your face is neither pointing up nor down. It is recommended to look at a spot on the floor in front of you at an angle of 45 degrees.

2. You need to gather a test sample of how your body reacts when you are telling the truth versus when you are telling a lie, and when you are thinking a thought that feels good versus a thought that feels bad. The muscle responses to these two situations become the benchmark against which you can

compare your responses to statements of beliefs that you wish to change.

3. In order to test a statement you lift an arm and hold it straight but relaxed at a 90 degree angle from your body. The facilitator will apply gentle pressure with their first two fingers pressing down on your wrist. The idea is that when you tell a truth or make a statement from a place on the emotional scale above the worry line your body is stronger and when the facilitator applies pressure on your wrist your arm will not be displaced much at all, but when you tell a lie or make a statement from a place below the worry line, your arm will be displaced a longer distance. When the facilitator applies pressure, do not apply counter force or push back consciously. It is recommended that the facilitator say the words "be strong" as they apply pressure on your wrist because this amplifies the feeling of weakness if there is a weakness and allows you to do the work in order to create a positive shift.

4. The first test is easy. We test strength by telling a truth. By saying "my name is (your correct name first and last)" out aloud. The facilitator says "be strong" and applies pressure on your wrist. Both of you benchmark the reaction of your physical body in terms of the displacement felt. Then we test for how a lie feels in your physical body. So go ahead pick a friend or a movie star or a politician and call yourself by their name: "my name is (movie star)", facilitator applies pressure and you both feel the displacement and benchmark it. Some people

exhibit a wide displacement and others don't. The only important thing is to feel how your response is different from when you were telling the truth.

5. Now close your eyes and go to past positive to recall an event, person or thing that makes you feel really good, like a 10 on the emotional scale, when you're there nod your head so that the facilitator can proceed with the test. No need to tell the facilitator what you are thinking. Benchmark. Repeat with going past negative, benchmark. Now you are really to test for beliefs.

6. In order to check whether you truly believe something all you have to do is to test it, if it feels strong, then it is a statement that you believe in and if you test weak then it is a statement that you don't really believe in.

7. I recommend muscle testing for each statement of belief under the category of fears and challenges before doing the Four Step Process and again after completing it.

8. I also recommend muscle testing for the following statements representing the four aspects of our lives that cover all subjects:
   a. Money: Money flows easily to me; I have all the money I need for all the things I want.
   b. Relationships: I feel ease and harmony in all my relationships; I bring love and joy to everyone including myself.
   c. Health: My body is perfect in every way and it knows what to do to help me maintain my

physical well-being. I listen to my body and the guidance it sends my way.

d. Self-esteem: I love myself, I am one with everyone, no one is better than me or worse than me, we are all the same.

9. These broad tests will indicate to you those areas in your life where improvement would be nice to have.

In my experience the muscle testing technique shown here is helpful as a guide to indicate to us areas of our life where we need to do the vibrational work. Some people like to use a finger test, a pendulum or a body pendulum as a substitute for muscle testing. They do this mostly because a facilitator is not always available. These tests are just a guide – they don't have to be exact and they are certainly not absolute in the sense that testing for a statement or belief once doesn't square it away forever, because there is momentum associated with it. However, doing the muscle testing in conjunction with the Four Step Process makes the Four Step Process more powerful helping you to break the old momentum and the corresponding patterns in your life.

Our minds are powerful and our thoughts have the power to impact matter and give us the visible results we seek without creating the vibrational shift that we desire, and that is why I prefer doing the muscle testing with a facilitator as compared to doing it alone using another method.

FOUR STEP PROCESS
FOR RELATIONSHIPS

Let's keep working with the challenges and fears listed earlier to demonstrate the process.

The first statement under the category of fears is: My fear is that he doesn't care about me anymore. This is step one – the starting point for our exercise at the top of the page.

Step two is the end result we are looking for – it is usually the exact opposite of the statement in step one. We write this at the bottom of the page. For this example: I want my husband to demonstrate that he cares about me.

In step three we close the gap with softening, soothing statements, and in step four we use statements that are more directly pointing towards the end goal we wish to achieve.

This is how this exercise might look:

Step One: My fear is that he doesn't care about me anymore.

Step Three:

1. I know it feels like he doesn't care, but he's still here – we're still together. If we're still together that does count for something. (Now positive)
2. It's not just him, I've been so upset this last little while that I haven't been myself either. (Now positive)
3. I know he is really busy – I know he is always working. I do appreciate how hard he works. I guess he must be really tired by the time he gets home. (Now positive)

Step Four:

1. He still does his chores around the house – so he must care at some level. (Now positive)
2. He is so good with our children, I like that he cares for them – it gives us something common to care about. (Now positive)
3. We've had many good years together – we've had more good years than not. (Past positive)
4. We've been in many difficult situations in the past and always come through for each other. (Past positive)
5. I can remember how good it felt when we got married. I can recall all the wonderful times we've had together. There is a lot of strength in our relationship. (Past positive)
6. I've seen my friend Carol go through a similar situation, and it is wonderful to see how she and her husband worked things out and continue to be

happy. And I know so many people go through ups and downs and survive and thrive. If they can do it we can too. (Now positive)

7.   I think that both of us really want the same thing – we both want to be happy, and we both want love.

8.   I'm going to focus on visualizing us celebrating our next wedding anniversary with love and harmony. It makes me happy to think about it, and I am looking forward to both of us demonstrating affection for each other. I choose to trust that it will come to be. (Future positive)

Step Two: He cares about me and soon I will see signs that will confirm it. It will be nice to have him demonstrate that he cares about me.

Notice that the statements are all positive even though some are from the past, some are in the now and some are pointing towards the future. All of them soften the fear by providing a series of logical statements that create a possibility that the fear is untrue and that there might be another possibility, and that the possibility you want is actually realistic. The positive statements improve the level of vibration and as we go up the vibrational scale, the possibility of the future that we want actually turns into a probability. If we keep focusing this way the possibility will eventually become a certainty.

The Universe wants to deliver to us the way we want to feel, not the thing or person or event that we want – those are just by-products of the process. Sometimes we think we want a specific person in our lives, but the Universe knows that the happiness we are seeking lies with another. In such situations the process of alignment can result in the ending of one relationship and the beginning of another. As long as the ending comes from a place of alignment then we are still heading in the right direction – the direction of finding the feeling that we want to feel.

Four Step Process
for money

Step One: I am worried that I will not have enough money to meet all my expenses.

Step Three:

1. I have control over many things – I control how much I spend, and I know that I must keep a balance between what comes in and what goes out, and if I just relieve the stress of spending more than what comes in, then with time I will achieve the prosperity that I want. It is just the stress of spending more than what comes in that keeps the prosperity from coming. I can do that.
2. Even though it feels tough, I have done pretty well – I have managed to keep all my commitments so far.

Step Four:

1. I have achieved a lot. I own my own car, and I have a comfortable place to live.

2. I do have work and there is money coming in, and I am always on the lookout for new opportunities.
3. I appreciate my job, as it gives me a consistent amount of money that I can depend on.
4. I know that I am good at what I do and that with time the money that I want will come.
5. I know that there are many things I can do – skills that I can learn that I can start learning right away that will help me make progress.
6. I have seen others who were like me not very long ago make progress and achieve success, and if they can do it so can I.
7. I don't I need to hurry this process – everything is going really well for me. I am making progress, and that is the only important thing.
8. It is fun to think about all the things I will do in the future, and for now that is enough.
9. I am looking forward to feeling the improvement in my financial situation, and I can feel that improvement already. It feels good, it feels sure, it feels secure.
10. I am on my way to the prosperity that I seek, I will look for ways to enjoy my journey, and for now I am satisfied with my ability to keep all my commitments.

Step Two: My financial future is secure; I have more than enough money for all my needs and wants.

All we want to accomplish with this technique is to feel incrementally better. No need to look for physical evidence of improvement – just trust that if you are doing the work then the evidence will come.

THE MEDITATION SHORTCUT

The process of meditation is actually a wonderful shortcut that can take us up the emotional scale without having to do The Four Step Process. It works on the reverse principle that if we can just find a way to go up the emotional scale then a different and better set of possibilities will become available to us, and when we spend more time higher up, those possibilities become probabilities and finally manifest, and when the manifestation takes place, it enables us to give up the negative beliefs that were keeping it from coming – because the manifestation is proof that the negative belief was wrong and without foundation.

I often say in my meditation classes that you cannot tell your brain to stop thinking – it's like telling your heart to stop pumping blood. The organ is a part of the machinery of our physical body that keeps our body functioning the way it should; if we shut it down we cannot function. Make sense? So the objective of meditation is not to stop thought, it is in fact to gain control over our thinking process by choosing something small and emotionally unimportant to focus on, so that for a short period of time we stop thinking about all the things that keep us knotted up. Because it is our focus on those particular thoughts that keeps us at lower vibrational levels as soon as we turn our attention or focus away from them we naturally go up the emotional scale. A state of joy and happiness is supposed to be our natural state. When we are not in our natural state we experience discomfort or negative emotion. The role of the negative emotion is to let us know that we are no longer in our natural state so that we can do something to recover. But society teaches us otherwise. We learn as children that being "emotional" is inappropriate and if we have negative emotion we should brush it under the carpet or ignore it rather than heed the indication that it is giving us.

It's like fuel gauge on your car. When the fuel gauge says getting close to empty, do you ignore it? Put a happy face sticker on the gauge and keep driving? Of course not – you look for a gas station and fill up your fuel tank again – right? Well, it works the same way with the emotional scale. Negative emotion tells us that our tank of happy feelings is getting depleted. The action we need to take is to fill it up again, not to ignore it – because if we did ignore it pretty soon our car would stall, we would be stuck along the way, and have to walk a very long way on a very rough road to get back on track. Make sense?

So getting back to the subject of meditation - meditation does not mean no thought. In fact, it means focused thought. When we consciously make the decision to focus on something unimportant, to which we have no emotional attachment such as the sound of our breath as we breathe in and out, or counting as we breathe or focusing our attention on a candle, or the hum or the air conditioner or the sound of a dripping faucet or picture a beautiful beach or forest in our mind (as we do in guided meditations) we are focusing on a simple thought that has no negative strings attached to it. In the space of time that we are able to control our focus and keep it from wavering we are allowing our vibration to rise on the emotional scale and we can go up many steps on the emotional scale in one meditation session of fifteen to twenty minutes. This fifteen to twenty minutes is enough to create a little bit of pulling power or momentum going up the emotional scale. With repetition and daily practice our lives would keep changing and getting better – a little bit every day.

There is no right or wrong way to meditate and there is no such thing as a bad meditation. Meditation will always help to improve your vibration in the upward direction on the emotional scale.

With a daily practice of meditation you will start spending enough time in the higher vibrations that the set of possibilities at these levels will become vibrationally accessible to you. In the beginning you will start feeling just a little bit better about where you are in life – nothing will really change in your manifested reality that you can see or touch and feel or that others can see. But if you stay with it, then over a period of time physical manifestations will begin to show up, and your vibration will continue to improve as a result, so that you will automatically give up all your negative beliefs as you will have proven them to be wrong.

The Four Step Process works in the same way – taking you up the emotional scale in tiny steps. The difference between the way these two techniques work is that The Four Step Process involves conscious focus on the problem in order to change it around, while meditation involves focusing away from the problem in order to change it around. Neither one is better than the other. In my journey I have used both. Daily mediation is a part of my life – just like brushing my teeth, it is something that I do every day. When I first started working with the Law of Attraction and figured out how to do The Four Step Process, I worked with it on a daily basis. As a result, my thinking process has changed so that I have developed a habit of thinking my thoughts in a manner that keeps me above the worry line consistently. You will reach that place too – all it takes is practice.

When you start living your life above the worry line consistently, you will only need to dust off and use The Four Step Process on rare occasions for yourself, mostly you will find yourself teaching it to others.

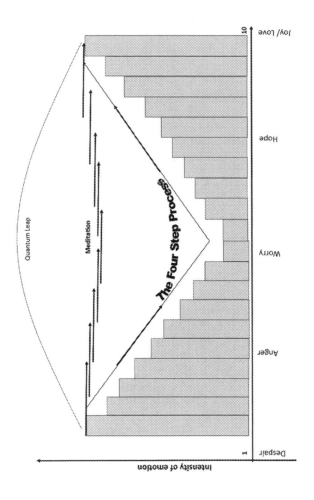

The answer to the question: "why me?"

What the preceding discussion boils down to is that our own habit of thought is our biggest obstacle. If we keep thinking our habitual thoughts like we always have, we will keep getting the results we have been getting in the past. It brings to mind the famous and often quoted words from Einstein "insanity is doing the same things over and over again, but expecting different results". I think it's more about thinking than doing, because any action we take is prompted by the thought that preceded it. So if we change our thoughts our results will change.

I discovered this golden truth by accident. Many years ago, I had a sales job based on one hundred percent commissions. It was tough – financially tough, not knowing if I would earn the money I needed in order to cover my mortgage payment and other expenses. Money was a huge issue back then. My work involved a lot of driving, and so I decided to start borrowing self-help audio books from the local library to keep me company and help me learn how others had gone from having very little to making it big, and listen to these all day as I drove around. I don't believe that I actually acted on anything in those audio tapes, but my life improved and things got better for me. As my understanding about how the Law of Attraction works improved, I began to understand that it was because of the fact that I had stopped thinking my own thoughts and focused on the positive words and suggestions contained in the audio books. Just that shift of focus was enough to allow the well-being that was lined up for me to start flowing into my life.

So the answer to the question: "why me? why do bad things happen to good people?" is simple – it is because they have a habit of thought that is destructive – it's a "thought addiction" based on the philosophy of telling it as it is, being realistic and logical to a fault and then seeking control by making things happen through physical effort based on logical arguments, rather than allowing things to happen based on emotional guidance and using action as a means to enjoying the journey as the path unfolds effortlessly.

In summary bad things happen to good people because one or more than one of the following variables apply to the way they think:

1. They follow their heads, they analyse, they make lists of pros and cons, and as a result they muddle up their vibration, going up and down the vibrational scale on the subject of their focus and not maintaining a clear focus at the top of the emotional scale which comes from looking at only the pros of a situation.

2. They take too much responsibility for everything they do as well as what others do and think, and as a result live most of their life at the lower levels of the emotional scale trying to please everyone but themselves, and that is why they don't have access to the possibilities that exist at the higher levels of the emotional scale.

3. They want others to understand their point of view and as a result focus on telling it as it is rather than telling it the way they want it to be. In addition, they try to find explanations that will help others understand and usually these explanations involve focusing on things in a way that is not conducive to being high on the emotional scale, because in that explanation they try to point out the pros in favour of their decisions and actions and in doing so they tend to list out the cons of the other options available to them and this muddles up their vibration so that it is not clearly pointing to the thing that they want.

4. They want to make everyone else happy before making themselves happy, not knowing that they cannot have access to the best possibilities which can only manifest from a place of joy on the emotional scale. When you're trying to find reasons to make others happy, you are taking responsibility for something you really have no control over and this creates needless stress.

5. They believe in trying hard at everything, and therefore they never learn the power of allowing things to happen. They feel that making things happen is equal to control, whereas true power is in

allowing things to happen by being relaxed about them.

6. They try to figure out the sequence of events that will be required in anything happening rather than allowing the Universe to find the best possible path – therefore they create probabilities that are not necessarily the best fit for what they wish to achieve. So they are always asking questions like "when? who? and how?

7. They feel that they should put happiness on hold until there is something to be happy about. In other words, they want to succeed first and get the object of their desire before allowing themselves to feel good, whereas the Law of Attraction is all about feeling good first so that things that you desire can come to you. They look for physical manifestation as the trophy or the success rather than the emotional feeling.

8. They have set ways of thinking about what is right or wrong, good or bad, and they measure themselves as well as others against this yardstick. So they feel good or bad based on events and manifestations rather than controlling how they feel so that the best things can come to them. A lot of times their standards of what is right or good comes from what other people have told them; family members, friends and the society at large. As a result, they ignore the guidance that they have inside them or they interpret it incorrectly. When they feel a negative emotion such as anger or revenge, rather than using it as guidance about where they are on the emotional scale they feel that they are being

inappropriate and therefore they suppress the emotion rather than using it as a bench mark for thinking the sort of thoughts that will take them up the emotional scale. Sometimes, they think that when they feel a negative emotion it is guidance telling them that the thing they want is bad for them in some way, whereas what it really means is that they are not vibrationally lined up on the emotional scale in a way that will line up with the thing that they want.

9. They are mostly dis-satisfied with where they are in life, and comparing themselves with others unfavourably. Any sort of comparison will always take you down on the emotional scale, because when you call yourself less than another you feel bad and when you call someone else less than you, you feel bad. When you feel bad you cannot maintain a position that is high on the emotional scale, so you cannot have access to all the possibilities that are lined up to manifest at the level of joy.

If you were nodding your head while reading the above list and saying "sounds familiar", I want you to know from the bottom of my heart, that it's Ok. Nothing has gone terribly wrong that you cannot fix. All is well. It doesn't matter that you learnt to do things one way, because you can always learn to do them another way. The important thing is to be open to change, and to know that if others like you have been able to turn things around, you can do so too. Let me share a secret with you: all those nine points above – they were all true for me, yes, each and every one of them was me, and that is why I was the one asking the question "why me?" on many occasions in my life. If any of the points above are you, all you have to do is to stop doing the thing that you're doing that keeps you at the lower vibrations, and you will automatically rise up the emotional scale because that's what our natural state of being is – we are happy people. You can also go back to the section about The Four Step Process and use it to shift your vibration on any subject.

Here's another technique that helped me turn things around. When confronted with things that didn't feel good, I started asking myself the question "do I want to be a sponge or a duck?". The logic behind my thinking was that a sponge absorbs everything and that when I am like a sponge I absorb things that hurt me such as other people's negative opinion about me or things that concern me, things that are going on in the world, what people are saying and doing, and where I am focusing. When I am a sponge I absorb worry by focusing on things that cause me to worry. Like a sponge I will sink to the bottom of the pond after I have absorbed all the water I can possibly contain. When I can take no more worry than I have already absorbed I sink to the bottom of the emotional scale, and there I will stay until and unless I find a way to wring out all the water. Sometimes, someone will appear like a mentor or a teacher or a book who will inspire me to reach for the surface of the pond again. They are transient, in the sense that they don't stay with me for very long, so I must find a way to stay afloat on the surface of the pond all by myself. That's what ducks do. The world can throw whatever it likes at them, they just shake their feathers and allow it all to fall off – they absorb nothing and so they are able to stay afloat on the surface of the pond at will. Make sense? So when I ask the question: "do I want to be a sponge or a duck?" it's a reminder to me to do those things that will allow me to stay afloat at the higher end of the emotional scale.

It's rather fun to think of things this way because when you're in a conversation with other people you can think about being a duck and shift your attention to that. Let me give you an example. Let's say I'm with a group of friends, and they start talking in deprecating ways about another friend that we all know – what should I do? Should I try to change their opinion? No. That won't go well, because I will be "trying" to change their opinion – and where there is effort involved, the direction on the emotional scale is downward, because when you "try" you are not allowing – making things happen is a very different feeling from allowing things to happen.

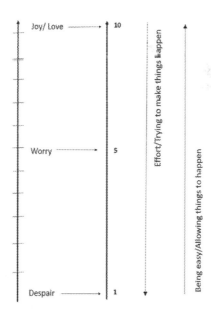

Ok, so we have established that the easier thing to do is to not try to change their opinion, and allowing is all about taking the easy path. Now I have a couple of options:

1. I can let them chatter away, while I turn my attention to something else and "space out" with no concern for what they might think of my non-participation. This is an effective way of disengaging myself from the conversation.

2. I can nod at appropriate times in the conversation while I start my own head chatter saying things that soothe me about what is going on around me, for example, I could say "my dear friends don't really know what they are doing. They don't understand that this talk hurts them, but I don't have to teach them right now, they will learn when they are ready to learn. All I have to do is to send them my love and see them the way I want them to be. I know that all they are doing is to give birth to new desires about the way they want things to be". Thinking these thoughts makes me feel better so it helps me to maintain my position at a better place on the emotional scale.

3. I can say something aloud like "never mind him/ her, let's talk about something more interesting" and continue talking firmly changing the topic by telling my friends a story about something and making it interesting enough that I can divert their attention.

4. I can start making a list of things I appreciate about my friends. Appreciating in the now always has a

way of improving our vibration, plus my focus is now diverted to something other than the topic of conversation.

Which one of the options I choose to go with in the moment depends on which one seems the easiest route, that involves the least amount of work. None of the options are better than the other. In fact, if I did end up joining the conversation – would that be the end of the world? Would I cause something bad to happen in my world by this little of a slip? Not really – because I know what to do to get my vibration back up again. Besides, no one can keep their vibration constantly at one place on the emotional scale. Even during the course of one day we all move up and down the scale depending on what is happening around us and how we are thinking about it. Once, I understood that I was in control and I could always raise my vibration using appreciation and meditation, I was home free. Nothing could faze me anymore because I knew how to find my way up the emotional scale and that is the only thing that matters because it opens up all the wonderful possibilities that are not accessible from the lower levels of the emotional scale.

Now going back to the question: "why me?" The most important thing to understand is that the Universe or that which we call God has a very fair system for giving people the things they want. The system is based simply on trust and the Law of Attraction. When we trust that God loves us and gives us everything we want, then we have no reason to be unhappy or experience any negative emotion which takes us to the lower levels on the emotional scale. As a result, we have access to many wonderful possibilities from the field of all possibilities, and we manifest things, people and events that will make us happy. When we are lacking in trust that is when we ask questions like "when will I get what I want?", "why is it taking so long?", "how is it going to happen?", "why do those people have what I want and I don't?" and similar other questions that take us down the emotional scale, holding us back from all the things that we want to manifest that are only accessible at the higher vibrational levels.

Choosing to appreciate what is, is a way of demonstrating our trust in God and leads to the field of all possibilities opening up for us. God's system is fair, those who complain have more to complain about, and those who appreciate have more to appreciate about. This is the Law of Attraction. It is constant and steady and never changing and treats everyone the same way. This is what we call "faith". Law of Attraction is all about trust and faith in the Universe, in that which we call God. Therefore it is to our benefit to learn how the Law of Attraction works and start using it to our advantage at a conscious level. And the only reason that bad things happen to good people is because they are so busy reaching for the things they want that they forget to appreciate the things they already have. They think that they are positive minded because they want positive results but for the most part their thoughts, words and actions are focused on what isn't working in their lives and what they want to change. And that, my friends, is why bad things happen to good people.

As I look back on my life at all the times when I thought the Man Upstairs wasn't being fair to me, I can see that He was absolutely fair, because it wasn't about what I deserved, it was about how I thought about what I deserved.

Abraham-Hicks use a powerful analogy about the power of one happy stick. You can read about it in more detail in the book Abraham 101. In summary, what it means is "one bad apple spoils the whole bushel". We have the choice to direct our power of focus on the bad apple or the thing in our life that isn't working quite the way we want it to, and it will pull everything into it so that over a period of time even those things that are working will no longer work. You see, it's true that "where attention goes, energy flows" because when you give attention to what is not working you bring yourself to the lower levels of the emotional scale and when that happens the people, events and things that were available to you from a higher place on the emotional scale are no longer within your vibrational reach, so all subjects in your life suffer as a result.

On the other hand, we can focus on all the things that are working and the positive momentum that will be created as a result will sweep the one bad apple out of the bushel, in other words the thing that was not working before will receive the positive energy that will allow it to be settled to our advantage. This is because when we appreciate all the things in our life that are working the positive energy that is generated results in our going up the emotional scale and opens up the corresponding set of possibilities for everything in our life. That's why the saying goes "the better it gets, the better it gets".

WHAT ABOUT SUBCONSCIOUS THOUGHTS?

When I share my perspective about how we think our thoughts and what happens to us as a result, I invariably get asked "but what about the things we do unconsciously or without thinking?"

The thing to understand is that an action that seems unconscious or driven by our subconscious mind does not start out being that way. It is a series of thoughts that are thought and acted upon, that create a momentum. Once the momentum of thought-action is well established, the action continues without needing the thought to energize it. You see, thought is the energy that feeds the action. It's like the mill I used to visit with my mother when I was a kid. The men who ran the mill had to exert a lot of energy to push the wheel in order to get the big milling rock to start turning. As a child I was fascinated by the fact that once the wheel was going really fast, all the men had to do to keep it going was to tap it gently – they did not need to exert any force. However, when they wanted to stop the wheel, they would have to either let its momentum peter out or they would have to exert force to make it stop. I can relate that to the way we think our thoughts and the actions that follow. When a thought is thought repeatedly and followed by a specific action, then after a while it turns into a habit, and we don't really need to do anything to keep it going. That's when we do things "unconsciously" or unawares or on autopilot. If the resulting action is something good, like driving a car (which is pretty much on autopilot once you have enough practice with the gears and the accelerator) then we don't need to do anything to bring the momentum of knowing how to drive to a halt, but if it is something undesirable such as alcohol addiction then we have two choices, we can exert force to stop the momentum by making the conscious effort to break the habit or we can let the momentum peter out by going cold turkey for three days or more.

Beliefs are just thoughts we think repeatedly; in other words they are thoughts with momentum. That's why it seems as if beliefs are in our sub-conscious. When we accept the relationship between cause and effect to be true, then every time we make a decision that is in keeping with it we are feeding the momentum of it (like tapping the milling stone) and making it stronger, until it reaches a point where the momentum of a belief is so strong that we cannot act cross ways to it.

Only those beliefs play a role in our lives that have momentum because they are still active in our lives. For example, for me, the belief that sugar is bad has momentum. It is a well learned belief, and information that proves it right always comes to me. On the other hand, I no longer believe that a black cat crossing my path means bad luck – I have disproved that one and so it's momentum in my life has petered out. If a black cat did happen to cross my path it would have no impact on my day.

The next question I get asked on this subject is about "gut feel" or "sixth sense". Most people agree that we have some form of guidance through our sixth sense, I hear people say things like "my sixth sense was telling me that this thing was bad for me". Most people also believe that this sixth sense is controlled by their sub-conscious mind, and that we have a greater knowing of things at the sub-conscious level. It is not uncommon to hear people say "I must have known that sub-consciously", or "I can't get rid of that fear because it is in my sub-conscious". The subject of guidance from gut feel and that of the sub-conscious are two very different subjects, even though they seem connected.

Guidance from the gut feel is really our emotional GPS helping us to make the right decisions. But how do we interpret this guidance? When something doesn't feel right, does that mean it is bad for us? In my observation, that is how most of us treat this guidance. If it feels bad, it is bad, and once we attach that label to something or someone we usually stick to it. A more precise interpretation of this guidance signal is: if it feels bad, I'm not vibrationally ready or lined up with it.

I think this is an important distinction because we can make the decision to line-up with something and do the vibrational work required in order to align ourselves with it, and if we do, then that thing that feels bad will no longer feel bad. For example, Charlie wants to ask Alex for a date, but every time he thinks about it he feels uncomfortable. Charlie can decide that because he feels uncomfortable that it is just not possible for him to raise the question or Charlie can decide to close the vibrational gap with his self-talk and get himself to a place where he can ask Alex out.

We've all seen those movies where someone like Charlie moves up and down the emotional scale, being ready to ask for the date in one second and chickening out the next. But if he can hold his vibration steady in an attitude of hope and take action from that level on the emotional scale, the chances that he will get what he wants are high. It works that way with everything. Once we decide what we want we must stay lined up with it in order for our gut feel to send us a positive signal upon which we can act.

Let's take another example. Let's say that Charlie wants to take a vacation, but it feels a little bit out of his reach from where he stands. Every time Charlie thinks of booking it, it feels bad – but he really wants it. One day Charlie is walking along feeling really good, he passes by a travel agency with a big sign advertising a sale on a cruise. Charlie says to himself "that sounds like a good deal, it would be fun to find out more". With that thought in mind, Charlie steps into the shop and the rest is history, as they say. By the time he comes out, he has already booked himself for the cruise. Even while he is still in the shop, he is wondering "am I doing the right thing?" and the little voice in his head says "just put it on your credit card and worry about it later" – so that's exactly what he does. Only, his worry starts even before he leaves the shop. He starts thinking that he's taken on too much, how is he going to pay off the credit card. With each passing day the pressure mounts, as Charlie's financial situation is really tight to begin with, but his attention to the fact that he has booked the holiday makes it even worse, bringing him lower down on the emotional scale. In other words, Charlie is unable to raise his vibration to a level where he can feel good about having booked his trip. He keeps telling himself how stupid it was to act on the spur of the moment, but he doesn't want to cancel his trip either because he's told everyone about it – if he cancels what is he going to tell everyone? Under these conditions Charlie has reached a point where he must do something to feel relief, to feel a little bit better. In fact, every time he feels bad about his situation, he is really asking for improvement, so the pulling power of his desire to improve his money situation and be able to take that trip is extremely high. What is Charlie's gut feel trying to guide him towards?

Was his initial gut feel about booking the cruise wrong? And what is his gut feel telling him to do now?

Charlie's initial decision was made from a high place on the emotional scale. He was happy and so he attracted something that would make him happy. There was no mistake made, from where he was on the emotional scale booking the cruise was the right thing to do. If Charlie could have maintained a position high on the emotional scale other good things would have followed and he would have no cause for worry. Instead Charlie choose to look at

things going wrong in the future, and guess what he got –
things going wrong in the future.

From where he stands now Charlie has a couple of
alternatives:

1. He can continue with things the way they are and
   do nothing to improve his vibrational stance, in
   which case his financial situation will stay the way
   it is. He will go for his cruise and return with a
   bigger burden.
2. He can cancel his trip and get a refund. There
   may be some penalties but for the most part he
   will get his money back and feel more in control
   of his finances. On the downside, at some point
   in time he will have to tell his friends that he is no
   longer going on the cruise. This thought does not
   feel good because it makes him feel less than his
   friends.
3. He can do the vibrational work to improve his
   vibration and bring himself back into the feeling
   place from where he made the decision to book the
   cruise.

What do you think Charlie should do? What is the path of
least resistance?

The way to figure that out is to play the three scenarios out
into the future.

1. If things stay the way they are or get worse – how will it feel? Pretty bad. On a scale of one to ten, it would feel let's say like a three or a two.

2. If he cancels his trip and get the money back that will feel a lot better than the way he is feeling just now – probably at a five or a six. The thought of having to back out and telling his friends would probably bring him down from a six to a four.

3. Charlie could do the vibrational work in order to improve how he feels about his situation. If he could hold this position for parts of the day, slowly he would start to build momentum on this alternative and then a corresponding set of possibilities would open up for him. This choice ranks high on the emotional scale but low on momentum.

4. Doing the vibrational work and lining up with the cruise is possible, but Charlie is unable to keep his focus on it because the vibrational gap is so wide. From where he stands the possibility of his money situation improving fast enough seems impossible to him and so every time he turns his attention to the cruise he feels bad about following his impulse and in the process he makes the problem bigger. Thinking about going on a cruise really should make him happy so that he feels like a ten when he visits this subject but in reality he feels like a two or a one. He tries to do the vibrational work and it does help in the moment but it only takes him from a one on the emotional scale to a two or a three.

When we put these options on the emotional scale it's easy to see which one is the path of least resistance. There is an important distinction here because the path that is the easiest to travel is the path that has the most momentum. A path that has the most momentum is the path that has been thought about the most; this does not necessarily make it the path that will yield the best results. In Charlie's case the path that is the easiest to travel is Option number one – status quo, where his financial situation stays the same at best. Because Charlie has been thinking about his money situation and worrying about it for a while, he has been focusing there and so it has become a habit – it is easy for his thoughts to go there, and therefore the momentum is high, but he feels bad about his situation so it scores low on the emotional scale.

If Charlie doesn't take any action at all, then the path of least resistance or Option one will go from being a possibility to a probability to a certainty. It seems as if this option manifests that something unwanted will have happened, but in reality nothing will have gone wrong. By manifesting option one Charlie will give up all his worry about money and when he does so, Source will be able to lead him towards that which he really wants. As discussed earlier, sometimes the path to the things we want is not a straight line, it is a winding road with a varied terrain that is not always a smooth or fast ride.

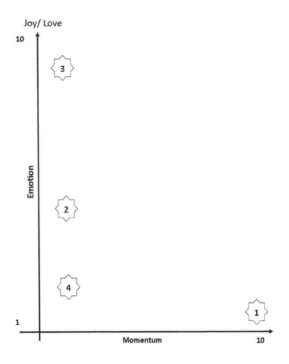

Charlie can decide to do the vibrational work using The Four Step Process to build momentum on Option number three which has the highest emotional score but the lowest momentum. Doing the vibrational work will get momentum started and with practice get it going faster and faster so that Option three will become a probability and then a certainty. Sometimes, when we start using the Law of Attraction deliberately we find it hard to maintain our focus in a place that it is not used to being, so closing the vibrational gap takes more time and more effort. But with practice the gap can be closed, and once you get a taste for being able to close the gap at will you start feeling that you have real and absolute control over your life. It's a lot like when people first start going to the gym because their personal fitness has got to a point where it cannot be ignored – they would much rather not have to go, the thought of staying home to watch television feels a lot better than going to the gym, because that thought has a lot more momentum. Some people give in to the momentum but others go to the gym despite the fact that they don't feel like it. When they go, they feel better because keeping a commitment (especially a commitment to yourself) feels good, it feels like allowing. Breaking a commitment has resistance because it feels hard, and takes work, but if the thought of staying at home has high momentum, then it feels easier to take that route. The next day you feel bad that you didn't go, and that focuses on the problem and makes it worse. If you did go, then most likely your muscles would be aching the next day; that's almost representative of the emotional stretch to close the vibrational gap. The first few days of going to the gym won't be easy – the television will keep calling you; but one day you will reach a point where going to the gym and working out will have a very high momentum – a momentum that surpasses watching television, and from that point on it will be much easier to say "no" to television. Now if your friends call you to come and hang out with them, the momentum of going to the gym will be so high that it will be easy for you to tell them, "I love you very much, but I can't miss a day at the gym". This is the "slight edge" principle that Jeff Oleson talks about in his book also called The Slight Edge. That's what Susan Jeffers means when she says "Feel the fear and do it anyway", because when you first try to deviate from the status quo, it's hard because the momentum keeps pulling you back and you have to apply great effort in order to change and start doing things differently.

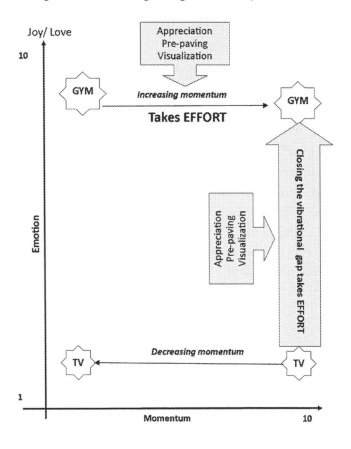

In terms of the Four Step Process described earlier, when you have high intensity of emotion or momentum about not looking or feeling good in your physical body, your momentum score is 10 but your emotion score is 2 – this is Step One: you know what you don't want.

Step Two is the opposite of Step One. In other words, you want to look and feel good in your physical body. What coordinates on the chart correspond to this desire? Well, you would probably have to be somewhere between 7 and 10 on the emotional scale as well as 7 to 10 on momentum in order for this desire to manifest. The difference between the two is the vibrational gap that needs to be closed. How do you close the vibrational gap?

Step Three: you reduce the negative momentum by saying soothing things to yourself so that you feel a little better, and you go outside your comfort zone of watching TV every night in order to go to the gym.

Step Four: appreciating where you are and what you are doing, pre-paving and appreciating going to the gym saying things like "I'm doing the right things, my physical body is benefiting from the exercise, pretty soon I will start seeing the results of my work", and visualizing or seeing yourself looking and feeling good. Slowly the momentum of these positive thoughts increases and the manifested results indicating that the vibrational work you are doing start showing up.

Have you ever come across those people who go for regular walks and eat very little, but are still over weight? I have. And the missing ingredient in the physical work that they are doing is appreciation. They never shift their focus from what they don't want so the negative momentum that they have going on never peters out. At the same time they get on a diet and start generating positive expectations, and positive momentum – now they have what Abraham-Hickscalls split energy in the sense that they have both what they want and what they don't want equally active in their vibration so that there is no clear pull in one direction. This split energy is draining and feels really bad. Eventually they give up on the diet and say that it doesn't work. The same example applies to almost everything else in life. When someone has a job that they don't like, or a family member they would much rather not have, and things never seem to get better, it's because they have that split energy going on. Making long list of pros and cons for anything does the same thing – it gives you split energy. The only difference is when you make a decision and move on, now you have stopped splitting your energy and as long as you keep appreciating the decision you have made things will work out amazingly for you.

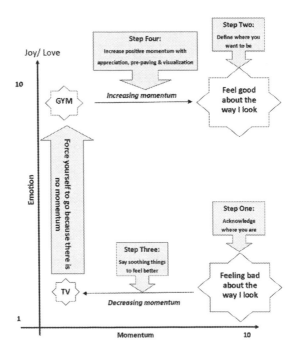

Let's go back to Charlie and his cruise. Because the vibrational gap is the largest for Option number three, it might be easier for Charlie to pick Option number two and line-up with it. The more he thinks about this alternative and gives it his energy, the more momentum will build up until he will reach a point where it feels really easy to him to go and get a refund and be able to deal with his friends.

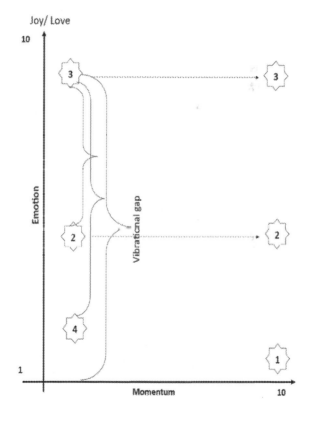

A lot of times when people refer to their gut feel they are really referring to momentum. We can feel momentum, because it is merely the speed of a thought. Momentum represents the pulling power of the thought. Momentum is what takes a possibility from the field of all possibilities and converts it into a probability and then converts the probability into a certainty. Momentum trumps everything. So the only way we can manifest something that is higher up on the emotional scale is by increasing its momentum from a point of view of having it. This is an important distinction because; as Abraham-Hicks would say "every subject is really two subjects – the having of it and the not having of it". When you focus on a subject from the point of view of having it then you are increasing the momentum of that outcome and when you focus on the subject from the point of view of not having it, then you increase the momentum of that. In Charlie's case, what he really wants is ease and flow on the subject of money (a perspective of having it, or going to the park), the opposite of it is the lack of money, which is what he keeps thinking about because that is what his reality is. That's how things get worse. We focus on a subject because we want it to improve, but we think about the "fact" that we cannot see an improvement and when we do that we increase the momentum of lack. We have to slow down or break negative momentum in order for things to change. Momentum of thoughts is the variable that prioritizes what the future will hold. Subjects with a higher momentum have higher manifestation priority. The Universe is fair, it doesn't care about how much you want something, it measures your wanting by the amount of attention or momentum you give to a subject, so if you look at something from a point of view of lack more often than the point of view of having it – you are really telling the Universe that you want more of the lack of it in your life.

Think about it. The reason that the planets revolve around the sun is momentum. The reason the Earth revolves on it's axis is momentum. Once a momentum is established it takes a long time for it to peter out on its own, but when an effort is made to introduce another force into the mix, the momentum can be slowed down and turned around. All the laws of physics apply to thought energy in the same manner that they apply to any other form of energy, which is why quantum physics is closing the gap between science and spirituality. I'm no scientist, but that's what makes sense to me anyway.

The bottom line is, if we want to master the art and science of deliberate creation based on the Law of Attraction, we need to focus our effort on controlling the process through which we give birth to our thoughts. This involves:

1. Focusing on the way we want to feel rather than the thing/person/event we wish to manifest.
2. Finding things to appreciate that will help us to feel the way we want to feel.
3. Focusing on the right perspective (lack vs having).
4. Using the right words to formulate our thoughts because words reflect beliefs.
5. Enjoy being in the now, and let the Universe take care of the future, rather than exerting effort to make things happen in the future.

ABUSE AND ADDICTION

All abuse and addiction are about momentum. Someone who is prone to an unhealthy habit of any sort, merely has a lot of momentum going on at a level below the worry line. This momentum is so strong that even though at an intellectual level they understand that their habit is not doing them any good, yet they cannot buck it's current. Smokers and alcoholics display momentum all the time.

In these situations, it is possible to go cold turkey, and within a few days the negative momentum will subside to a level where it does not sweep them up any more. Side by side a new, positive and empowering habit can be initiated which over time will gather momentum so that the individual concerned never feels the urge to return to old ways.

When people relapse into old patterns all it means is that the old momentum may have been reduced but it did not completely peter out, and that somewhere in their thinking the individual was feeding it by giving it attention and thinking about it.

The next time you witness someone who is being swept up in the momentum of a habit that does not serve them, send them your love. Know that they are hurting badly because no one would hurt themselves if they could help it – they are victims of momentum. They don't know how to deal with the momentum and to break its hold on them. Sometimes, a major life event will jolt them in a way that shifts their focus for long enough to allow the old momentum to dissipate – in other words a quantum leap. Sometimes an individual will appear as a mentor who will help them to break the old momentum and help them to shift their focus in a way that creates a stronger positive momentum in their lives. And sometimes, they will reach a stage where they are willing to do the vibrational work because being happy is so important.

Either way, if you have someone like this in your life you are no good to them if you focus on their problem, because by doing so you will just be adding your thought energy to the negative momentum and therefore make the problem bigger. Instead, see your friend the way you want them to be and give your thought energy to that image of them – activate that and add momentum to that, because that is what will truly help them to be who they really are.

GOALS AND
DEADLINES

Traditional goal setting teaches us to be specific about what we want, describe it in detail and set a deadline by which we want to achieve it. Many teachers of the Law of Attraction also teach the same thing.

It has always amazed me how some people say that just the process of setting up the goals contributed to their success and achievement, while for other people it had no impact. Some people will say "I asked for a new car by Christmas and I got it just in time" and other people will say "I asked for a new car by Christmas two years ago and I'm still waiting – where's my stuff?"

I know now that getting specific doesn't work all the time because it is only one side of the coin. The coin has two sides: one side is specific and the other side is general. Being specific works for some people, while being general works for others.

Who should be specific and who should be general? The answer is: if you're feeling good about the achievement of your goal, then you are heading up the emotional scale and creating momentum towards it, and in this situation the higher you go and the more momentum you create the more specific you can get. Getting specific on a goal creates acceleration towards manifestation (things go from possibility to probability to certainty faster) from a position that is high both on momentum as well as high on the emotional scale.

Some people know what they want in detail, but most of us start out knowing what we want in general and as we get closer to our goals we automatically get more specific. If you try to get specific when you are too far away from your goal on the emotional scale, you push your goal further away into the future. Because every time you visit your goal and observe that it has not been achieved you activate the vibration of "not there yet", which perpetuates "not there yet".

Putting a timeline on when you want things to happen is in the direction of getting specific. When you leave time out of the equation you are more general. For example, saying "I want to lose 30 pounds by December 31st of this year" is a lot more specific compared to saying "I want to lose 30 pounds". But when you have already lost the first 25 pounds and you are sitting in October, feeling really good about your accomplishment, then making the statement "I want to lose 30 pounds by December 31st of this year" feels more like a certainty and you can start getting more and more specific about it by visualizing yourself wearing the clothes that you would buy in order to enjoy your new look, and feeling how you would feel when people that you know compliment you on your accomplishment – doing so would increase the momentum for you from a place high on the emotional scale and you would be well on your way – you would feel the certainty of it in your physical body – you would know that it is a done thing.

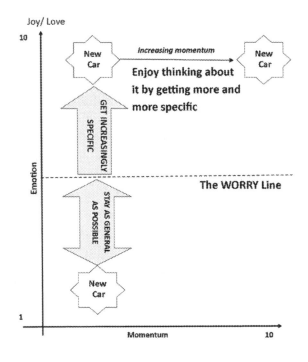

The only time done things slip away is when we shift our attention to some subject that takes us to an emotional place that is below the worry line. Any subject that we pay attention to can do this whether it has to do with us directly or not. For example, you can be at a place of complete joy getting closer and closer to what you want and then you might pay attention to a news piece about an event that happens somewhere in the world that makes you feel angry. Then you meet with others who express their anger on the incident, which magnifies the anger you are feeling. The next day you read the details in the newspaper and it magnifies your anger further. Everywhere you go people are talking about it and as you eavesdrop on their conversations you feel worse thinking thoughts like "why do things like this have to happen", "someone should do something about it" etc., not realizing that all of this is leading to your losing your place on the emotional scale and falling below the worry line. Your being below the worry line will impact all subjects in your life. As Abraham-Hickssay "nothing is more important than that you feel good".

INTERACTING
WITH OTHERS

People come into our lives in the same manner as other things – we attract them based on the way we think, the momentum of our thoughts and our place on the emotional scale. The powerful Law of Attraction matches us up with those who are vibrating on the same level of the emotional scale as us, or with the aspect of other's personality that matches where we are on the emotional scale. Let me explain more fully.

We have two types of people in our lives: those to whom we are bound by a relationship such as birth or marriage, and those to whom we are not bound in any way such as our colleagues at work, friends, neighbours and people from whom we purchase goods and services.

Those who are not bound to us in any way come into our lives and leave based on where we are on the emotional scale and where they are on a consistent daily basis. Those who are on a different emotional plane from us don't have access to us nor we to them. Even if we know them and go looking for them they will zig when we zag so that we will not connect with them unless we are on the same vibrational wavelength or level on the emotional scale. For example, let's say Charlie has a pipe leak under his sink. He tries to fix it himself, but it doesn't work. By this time he is feeling frustrated (he had a choice to make light of it instead of being frustrated). He goes to the hardware store to find a solution, but no one is able to give him any pointers (because instead of clearing up his vibration before going, he has gone there in a state of frustration). By the time he comes back home the leak has created a large puddle in the middle of the kitchen floor. Now Charlie is irritated (again he had a choice, he could have made light of it). He calls a few friends to see if anyone will recommend a good plumber or give him a few tips on what to do, but no one seems to be around to take his calls (because he hasn't cleared up his vibration nothing is going his way). Charlie finds himself getting angry (making things worse, he had a choice he could have soothed himself and kept calm). He goes to an internet directory and pulls a name, but no one seems to be there to take his call (because he hasn't cleared his vibration, things are not going easy for him). He keeps moving down the list getting more and more upset (negative momentum has a hold on him now), until finally he gets through to a plumber (he can only reach someone who is also on the same level as himself on the emotional scale. The plumber tells him that he can't come immediately and it will have to wait three days (another manifestation that is telling him that he needs to clear up his vibration – but he isn't paying attention). Charlie pleads his case and finally the plumber agrees to come out the next day for $50 extra. Charlie is really angry now that is having to spend $50 that he could have saved, but he has no other options (he had the choice again to look at this with appreciation and thinking that it was worth it to pay the extra money in order to get immediate attention, this would have helped him to feel better). The next day Charlie tells his colleagues about the horrible leak, and how he's being overcharged – he enjoys telling the story (because he has momentum on the subject, telling the story is easy; it is the path of least resistance). He even calls his mother and his sister to tell them the story. They agree with him and share similar stories of things that have happened to them or to their friends at some point (they collectively add their negative power of focus to the situation thereby making it worse). Charlie tells them that he's not really sure how good this plumber is, and how he's worried whether the guy will actually be capable of doing a good job – what if he loses money and the leak still doesn't get fixed? (Charlie has already pre-paved or created a negative visualization). Next day Charlie waits for the plumber at the appointed time but no one shows up (the Universe is trying to tell Charlie that he needs to work on his vibration so that his manifestations may improve – but Charlie isn't listening). Charlie tries calling but to no avail (another negative manifestation, another way for the Universe to tell Charlie to do the vibrational work to go up the emotional scale and improve his manifestations). Finally the guy shows up two hours later – apologizes and gets to work. It doesn't take him long to plug the leak and he is on his way. Charlie feels bad having to pay him the extra $50.00, and he doesn't feel good even though the leak is fixed. The next day Charlie's colleagues ask him if the leak was fixed and of course he tells them all about how the plumber was late and laments having to pay extra (generating more negative momentum). His mother and sister call to ask if the leak is fixed and of course he repeats the whole story again (generating more negative momentum). For the next few days everyone who meets Charlie gets to hear his story (adding more momentum). A few weeks later the leak starts again… (how could it not with all the negative momentum that has built up and Charlie's negative belief about the quality of the work he paid for) and Charlie starts the whole cycle again.

The rest of Charlie's life looks exactly like the water leak. Can you see why? Do you see how Charlie attracts people who are on the lower rungs of the emotional scale just like him? It is very likely that the same plumber has the capacity to do excellent work for someone else, but on the day Charlie got a hold of him, the plumber was having a bad day, and so they were both on the same level on the emotional scale – all the other plumbers who were on higher levels on the emotional scale and would have done a better job of fixing the leak without charging extra were unavailable to Charlie because of where he himself was on the emotional scale. Is it not clear from his behaviour why he was at a low level on the emotional scale and why he has momentum that is hard to break? Just look at all the times he goes to the dump in the way he thinks and talks. If Charlie had kept his position high up on the emotional scale even a usually bad plumber would have given him excellent service that day.

When my father came to visit with me in Canada he used to worry about the fact that his doctors were back home in Pakistan, and that if he had to go to the hospital in Canada he might end up with an incompetent doctor who would not be able to save his life. I would always tell him that if he was meant to live then the most incompetent doctor would be able to save him and if he was meant to die then the best doctor in the world would not be able to save him.

In relationships where we are bound to people, we can't avoid them, because we live with them or are in close proximity to them, nevertheless the Law of Attraction is still at play – in fact, it never stops, and so the fact is that our interactions are a reflection of where we are on the emotional scale. If people are nice to you, it is a manifested indication of the fact that you are above the worry line on the emotional scale and if people are not nice to you, it is a confirmation of the fact that you are below the worry line on the emotional scale.

I hear people say time and time again that they don't understand why so and so says hurtful things to them. There is only one answer. It happens because you attracted it as a result of being on the same vibrational level on the emotional scale with that experience at that moment in time. The way people treat us is a mirror that tells us our position on the emotional scale – it is guidance that is telling us where we are and where we need to go. It's telling us that we need to do the vibrational work to go up the emotional scale where all the good stuff is.

The diagram below illustrates how we only have access to people on the same emotional level as us, even though they might be at that level due to different reasons. For example, one person might be feeling like a 2 because of financial difficulties, while another person might be feeling like a

2 due to health reasons, and they will be part of the same universe. An 8 will have access to an 8 and a 5 will have access to a 5. Someone who is at a 5 will not be able to co-create with someone who is an 8 at that moment in time, even if they live in the same house – they will leave each other alone. But no one consistently stays at the same emotional level because we are all responding to stimuli in our environment – most of us are not in the habit of managing our emotions and deliberately generating the way we wish to feel. Most of us feel a certain way in response to the stimuli in our environment. Regardless, the point I'm trying to make here is that someone who is generally a happy person spending a lot of their time at an 8 will experience dips in their vibration during the day in response to things they notice and preferences they give birth to and in those moments when they dip they will interact with people who are at a lower level on the emotional scale.

One of the most important aspects of our interaction with others is forgiveness. Forgiveness is not about other people it is about us and the way we feel and think our thoughts. You see, when we think thoughts corresponding to the emotions of blame, anger and revenge, we hurt ourselves because we can only think those thoughts from a position low on the emotional scale, and the possibilities available to us with respect to all aspects of our life now correspond to that level on the emotional scale while the rascal towards whom our emotions are directed go scot-free to live their lives from where ever they choose to on the emotional scale unaffected by the way we feel about them. Forgiveness allows us to let go of the resistance we are feeling – going from being a sponge to being a duck so that we can raise our vibration and go back up the emotional scale.

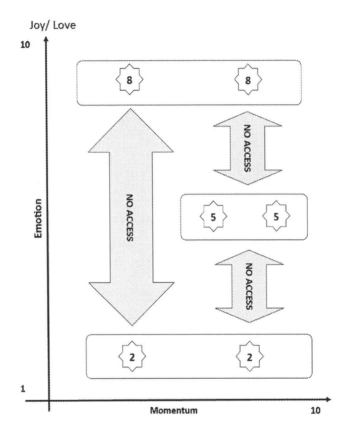

The process of forgiveness fits nicely with the Four Step Process. Step one: state how you feel about the person annoying you. Step two: state how you would like to feel. Step three: soothe yourself with respect to them and their behaviour. Step four: look for things to appreciate about the person. By the time you complete the process your vibration with respect to them will have shifted and that is all we are looking for – just a little shift every time you repeat the process.

Being able to forgive yourself for being imperfect, for having done whatever you have said and done is the most important form of forgiveness. I found that forgiving others was far easier than forgiving myself, and I learnt that guilt is a much lower vibration than blame. This was an important realization for me. I've gone from taking too much responsibility to blaming others and finally arriving at knowing that all of that was a waste of time and energy.

As a child I took it upon myself to be perfect. I liked it when my parents shined their love on me, and so I behaved in ways that would get me more of that. When they did not shine their light on me, it seemed to me that it was my fault that I was not "living" up to expectations and that was a bad thing. Trying to be perfect is a stressful job; it takes the fun out of things because you're not free anymore. The funny thing is, it wasn't my parents who asked me to be perfect – it was just something I took upon myself. I made the assumption that being loved was conditional upon being perfect. Somewhere along the line I forgot that love is love only when it is unconditional. When love is withheld based on the fulfilment of any sort of conditions it isn't love anymore, its emotional blackmail. I thought that it was my fault that I wasn't perfect. Being at fault creates a bad feeling, a feeling of blaming yourself, feeling inadequate or less than – feeling guilty. In order to change things around I used appreciation as my biggest tool. Learning to appreciate myself was a big step in the right direction. If you're like me and you can't find much to appreciate, focus on small things like appreciating your hands and feet, and your physical senses, and other aspects of your physical appearance and personality that are easy for you to appreciate. Ask those who are near you to tell you what they appreciate about you. Ask yourself how your inner-being would describe you, what would Source say about you. Louise Hay's mirror work is all about creating self-worth.

VISUALIZATION

Visualization is very much like meditation in the sense that it provides us with a short cut through the vibrational work. When we visualize, there is no need for us to probe for negative beliefs and flip them over. That being said, both meditation and visualization are much more effective when negative beliefs don't get in the way.

From where ever you are on the emotional scale you can create visualization or a day dream of where you want to be. The thing that makes visualization work as a tool is feeling the feeling rather than focusing on the tangible aspects of the thing you want.

Let's say you want a new car. You have two choices about how to visualize having got a new car:

1. You can visualize yourself in your new car, and see all the tangible details of what it looks like, what it sounds like, what it feels like; or
2. You can visualize yourself calling a friend or someone that you are close to and telling them how happy you are with the new car that you just got.

Zehra Mahoon

Both options are good and both options work, however, one works better than the other based on where you are on the emotional scale. Option 1 works better when you are above the worry line and Option 2 works regardless of where you are on the emotional scale. This is why when people start on a Law of Attraction journey, and meet teachers who tell them to do experiments in manifesting, those experiments don't always work across the board for everyone; they don't work for people who are getting specific about what they want to manifest from a place that is below the worry line on the emotional scale. Because when you are below the worry line getting specific about things actually magnifies the absence of the things you want and activates the absence of them in your vibration. The way to tell if you are getting too specific too soon is to notice how you feel. If it feels like an effort to specify all the minute details of what you want to manifest then it is likely that you are actually activating the opposite of what you want. Effort doesn't feel as good as ease and flow that is a natural result of travelling up the emotional scale towards love and joy and happiness.

I am personally in the habit of leaving things as general as possible. I have noticed that as I go up the emotional scale, I automatically start getting more specific and no effort is required – it feels exciting and natural to visualize the details of the thing I want.

The reason many teachers recommend that we visualize often is because doing so increases positive momentum. We only need to ask the Universe once, for it to be possible for us to get what we want. That's what the phrase "ask and it

184

is given" means. Asking again and again and feeling bad because we don't have what we want only magnifies the absence of it in our vibration and pushes it away – that's what traditional prayer does, and that is why so many are disillusioned with the process of praying and feel that God isn't really listening. Instead of praying, try visualizing, and do it just for the feeling of fun in experiencing all the things you want in your imagination rather than to make anything happen. When you do it just for the sake of feeling the feeling that's when you get the most effective results. So you see day dreaming is actually very good for you!

PRE-PAVING

Pre-paving is a process taught by Abraham-Hicks. For a more complete overview on it please refer to the book "Ask and it is Given" by Esther and Jerry Hicks. Pre-paving has become an important habit in my life and I believe it to carry immense value. I especially enjoy the night time and morning processes offered by Abraham Hicks in their book "Money and the Law of Attraction". For the purposes of our discussion, I will expand on my interpretation of the process of pre-paving.

Pre-paving is basically the process of preceding activity or taking action with vibrational work. Pre-paving involves focusing on the end result you wish to achieve, and making a clear statement that captures it.

For example, when I go to work in the morning, I will sit in my car outside my office just for a minute and say to myself "I want to have a good day today, I want to have fun, I want to do a good job, I want to co-create with my colleagues and my clients in harmony, I want to end the day feeling satisfied with my accomplishments".

What pre-paving does is that it gets us to focus on what we want to achieve, therefore activating it and creating a thought pathway towards it. It is an important ingredient that morphs possibilities into probabilities and certainties. It makes our emotional vibrational journey a lot smoother.

7 DAYS TO WELL-BEING

What it all boils down to is that we need to accomplish two things in order to live a magical life on an everyday basis:

1. Do the work in order to reach the higher levels of the emotional scale; and
2. Build momentum at these levels that will propel us towards all the things we desire.

Doing vibrational work is easy when you make the commitment to yourself that being happy is more important than anything else, because like all other things this work takes effort in the beginning. Sometimes people will make a commitment to do the work because they want to get a specific prize at the end of line – there is nothing wrong with that, but I do believe that it is more effective when you do the work with the objective of just feeling good and being happy in general, because all subjects in your life have to improve in order to give you that.

A seven day period of work is long enough to lay the basis of positive momentum and take you several notches up the emotional scale. That's not to say that you stop doing the work after seven days - in fact, the seven day period helps you to learn the exercises and start feeling what they do for you so that you can use them whenever needed, while some of them will become a permanent part of the way you live your life – at least that is what I have experienced.

Here is a list of things I have done in the past and continue to do on a daily basis in most cases – my daily routine.

1. When I am waking up in the morning, just in that space when I am not totally awake but sort of drifting in and out of wakefulness, I pre-pave my day using the morning intention by Abraham-Hicks from the book Money and the Law of Attraction. When I first started using the process, I would repeat it many times a day – I even have a CD in my car with the process that I listened to whenever I was driving – but nowadays repeating the process a couple of times while I drift in and out of sleep prior to waking up fully is sufficient to keep the momentum going strong.

2. Once I am out of bed, I get my morning coffee and spend a few moments appreciating it's aroma, and how it makes me feel – it's nice to get some positive momentum going first thing.

3. Next I like to sit in silent meditation for 15 to 20 minutes depending upon time constraints. I find that appreciation preceding meditation puts us in a higher place on the emotional scale and improves our meditation experience.

4. I usually come out of meditation and spend another five minutes with my eyes closed visualizing whatever it is that I am focused on improving that day. Meditation will usually leave a few notches higher on the emotional scale and therefore this is a perfect time to work on some visualization exercises.

5. When I first started turning my life around I would do a journal entry every day. Now a days I probably write once or twice a week. If I hit a low point, I will write everyday sometimes more than once a day. My journal entries are basically the Four Step Process done over and over and over again until I begin to feel back to my normal above-the-worry-line-self. In fact, it was through those months of daily journaling that the Four Step Process was born.

6. I look for things to appreciate – especially when I am not engaged in an activity that takes up my full attention. I especially enjoy appreciating my children, my cats and my trees.

7. I pre-pave all major blocks of time – sometimes just with one sentence, sometimes with more. I especially like to pre-pave interacting with others, loved ones as well as clients and eating a meal or doing a task that is important to me such as sitting down to write or cooking.

8. I listen to a teacher of the Law of Attraction every day, or read a passage from a book. I read and listen mostly to Abraham Hicks, but from time to time I enjoy other teachers as well.

9. I give each thing I do my undivided attention rather than multi-tasking. I find that I am more effective this way because my power of focus is not dispersed.

10. Half an hour of physical exercise or more depending upon the day. Physical exercise is important to keep the energy flowing through our bodies.

11. I repeat the night time process from the Abraham-Hicksbook Money and the Law of Attraction aloud every night.

More details on 7 days to well-being are available on my website zmahoon.com.

HAPPILY EVER AFTER

As a result of my journey I have developed a list of twelve habits based on the Law of Attraction that help me to make the most of the way I live my life. These are summarized below and a fuller discussion on them is contained in my book "Thrive: A Law of Attraction Guide to Creating a Successful and Happy Life".

1. **Appreciate and love**
   Appreciation, Appreciation, Appreciation. Appreciation really is the key to using the Law of Attraction deliberately. Ask yourself "what can I appreciate in this moment?"

2. **Feel for answers rather than think for answers**
   Learning to use the emotional guidance system, to be able to tell what feels good and what feels bad, and to be able to use the techniques explained in this book to raise your vibration at will, gives you immeasurable control over your life.

3. **Just say "yes" to whatever comes**
   This is about trusting that the Universe knows the path to everything that you want and if you will allow it, it will lead you there – sometimes through

the direct route and sometimes through an indirect route that might involve things that you think don't serve your purpose. Just trust that it all comes together in the end.

4. **How will this feel tomorrow?**

This is about recognizing that you have old momentum on some subjects that does not serve you anymore, and that breaking the momentum is going to take effort. Sometimes this means having to do things that don't feel comfortable in the beginning because there is no momentum on them, but once you make the effort to get the momentum going then it becomes easier and easier with each day, until the old momentum peters out and is replace by the new positive momentum.

5. **Stop offering explanations and advice**

When we try to explain our point of view to someone or give them the proper perspective on what we mean we invariably go to the past and tell them where we started our journey – this typically brings us down on the emotional scale, so there is really no need for it. People don't really need to know, and in most cases they don't care. Similarly, advice given and advice received are from the perspective of the person giving it, based on their understanding and experience of life not necessarily transferrable to your life. At times the Universe will use others to bring us an answer that we were seeking – it is easy to know the difference, for the one adds to confusion and the other adds to clarity.

6. **Choose wisely**

   We can make the conscious choice to accept or to deflect the beliefs that others share with us – we can choose our own belief system, once that gives us freedom and empowers us to have, be and do whatever we want.

7. **Stay focused**

   When we think of what we want and then worry and think that it may not happen we split our energy. This leads to our getting some of what we want mixed in with some of what we don't want. If we could control our power of focus so that it was unwaveringly pointed in the direction of the things we want, life would be far easier and we would accomplish a lot more and experience a lot more success.

8. **Pre-pave everything**

   Pre-paving is a way of maintaining our focus by clearly defining what we want. It is simple intentionality with the expectation that when you ask it is always given.

9. **Meditate**

   Meditation creates the pathway that allows guidance from Source to be heard by us. This is why when we practice meditation we create positive momentum in our lives so that all subjects in our life improve.

10. **Alignment before action**

    Recognizing when we are below the worry line on the emotional scale and curbing the momentum that urges us to act from that place leads to better decision making and more success. The only action we need to take is to do the work that will take us up the emotional scale and allow things to unfold rather than try to make them happen.

11. **Dream Big**

    A lot of us stop dreaming because we equate dreaming with setting up goals and if we have a history of not being able to get to our goals we start avoiding setting them up. But if we could step back and day dream just for the fun of it, in the same way that we enjoy watching a good movie – then we would feel better more of the time and then all things that we want would flow to us with ease.

12. **Stay General**

    Staying general and aiming for the way we want to feel rather than the specific thing or event that we would like leaves the door open for the Universe to bring us things that are better than what we asked for. If we get specific too soon we actually push away the very things that we want.

The 12 habits have an important place in my life – they have helped me to turn things around and start living life from a place higher on the emotional scale – all subjects in my life have improved as a result. If you are new to learning how to use the Law of Attraction deliberately, incorporate them in your life one by one, and consciously practice them in order to create momentum that is based on them. It doesn't take long to feel a difference, 7 to 10 days of consistent work will get your there, and then within the space of 30 to 40 days you will begin to feel a shift, you will feel happier and more in control, in one year your life will morph completely, and you will never be the same again.

It is my intention that this book leave you, the reader with a clear understanding of the Law of Attraction and how it works combined with strategies to put deliberate creation into action in your life. If this book serves you in such a manner do write a review or send me a note to let me know. Your feedback is the impetus I need to continue my work as an author and a speaker.

Much love and appreciation,

Zehra

About the Author

Zehra Mahoon lives in Ontario, Canada with her two beautiful children, Kinza and Faris, a hyper cat called Izzy and a lazy cat called Sitka. Zehra loves her home and her wooded backyard and the freedom she has in working from her home office. Over the past twelve years she has finally adjusted to the snow and cold weather in Ontario, but always welcomes a timely opportunity to get away to warmer places preferably with lots of old trees, rocks and water, good food and vibrant colours.

Zehra teaches weekly meditation classes at the local library. She loves to teach and write for her blog, as well as other journals and magazines. Zehra is an accomplished speaker and often makes television appearances. Aside from teaching the Law of Attraction, and offering financial advice, Zehra loves to cook and entertain and have fun with each new day of her life.

Zehra's other books include:

The Prosperity Puzzle: your relationship with money and how to improve it

Abraham 101: the basics of the Law of Attraction as taught by Abraham and understood by Me

If thoughts create then…how do people attract negative events they have never thought about? (free book available on <u>Zehra's blog</u>)

Is this apple from my tree: a Law of Attraction Guide for parents and grandparents.

Zehra's books are available in digital and print formats through Amazon.com

Some of Zehra's popular blog posts based on the Law of Attraction, include:

<u>Dream Big</u>

<u>Just say "Yes"</u>

<u>When people can't tell that they are being negative</u>

<u>How does it feel to win the lottery?</u>

<u>How beliefs are formed</u>

<u>For the love of food</u>

<u>Some Coaching Tips</u>

<u>Why does all hell break lose?</u>

<u>Can I get the man I want?</u>

One Last Thing...

If you enjoyed this book or found it useful I would truly appreciate it if you would post a short review on Amazon. Your support really does make a difference and I read all the reviews personally so I can get your feedback and make this book even better.

Much love and appreciation,

Zehra

Printed in the United States
By Bookmasters